SLOW COOKING

100 recipes for the slow cooker, the oven and the stove top

Antony Worrall Thompson

SLOW COOKING

100 recipes for the slow cooker, the oven and the stove top

Photography by Elizabeth Zeschin

MITCHELL BEAZLEY

To all those out there who have a slow cooker and are afraid to use it... And just as importantly, to those who don't, the hope that this book provides inspiration to invest in one.

Slow Cooking
Antony Worrall Thompson

First published in Great Britain in 2011 by Mitchell Beazley
An imprint of Octopus Publishing Group Ltd,
Endeavour House, 189 Shaftesbury Avenue, London, WC2H 8JY
www.octopusbooks.co.uk

An Hachette UK company www.hachette.co.uk

Distributed in the United States and Canada
by Hachette Book Group USA,
237 Park Avenue, New York, NY 10017 USA

ISBN 978-1-84533-641-7

Commissioning Editor Becca Spry
Deputy Art Director and Designer Yasia Williams-Leedham
Art Direction Juliette Norsworthy
Photographer Elizabeth Zeschin
Prop Stylist Isabel De Cordova
Home Economists Sara Lewis, Lorna Brash and Nicolas Ghirlando
Project Editor Georgina Atsiaris
Copy Editor Diona Murray-Evans
Proofreader Jo Richardson
Production Peter Hunt
Index Diana LeCore

Set in Original Garamond BT and Corbel
Printed and bound in China

Note:
Some models of slow cooker need
preheating; check the manufacturer's
instructions before preparing your dish.
All recipes in this book can be made using
a 4-quart working capacity slow cooker,
unless otherwise stated.

Contents

Introduction

Food trends come and go and then come back again, in one big circle. Occasionally, I hope that some trends disappear forever, as with nouvelle cuisine or pretty pictures on plates, which was all the rage in the 1980s. But sadly it's back in all but name. Now called molecular gastronomy, it involves a great element of science, but in essence it's pretty pictures on plates painted with tiny portions of pretentious food, but this time garnished with foams and "warm jellies" instead of the 80s' favorite, kiwi fruit.

I don't blame young chefs for wanting to be inventive. I did exactly the same in my youth, but when I look back at some of the dishes in my first book, *The Small & Beautiful Cookbook*, which was published in 1984, there are some repulsive combinations that should never be repeated.

Pretentious dishes are all about chefs giving customers food that the chefs want them to eat, rather than food that they, the customers, want to eat. I often wonder what these chefs eat when off duty; you can bet your bottom dollar it won't involve towers or foams. Experience tells me that chefs are partial to the occasional junk burger, a good juicy steak, or a bowl of a slow-cooked classic, such as Irish stew or cassoulet. Mashed potatoes or french fries would be their favorite potatoes, and often vegetables, but certainly salad, go by the board.

I'm a fan of the Slow Food movement, which was started in Italy in 1986 to counteract the invasion of junk food that was destroying the Italians' culinary heritage. There's nothing nicer on a cold day than a bowl full of steaming food: a soup, a stew, a pot roast, or a braise. Slow cooking has, of course, been around for centuries in various guises. From the bubbling cauldrons of the ancients to the present day when many Italians, French, Spanish, Greek, and Portuguese still bring casseroles of food mid-morning to the local baker, to use the turned-off bread ovens' residual heat to slow cook their dishes.

We have reached a crossroads in cooking. On the one hand is a group of chefs who are putting science back into food, using stabilizers such as xanthan gum and meat glues etc., and fancifying their dishes. And on the other, there are chefs intent on removing the spectacle of science from their food, and emphasizing instead the origins of their ingredients: by supporting the organic movement; respecting the seasonality of foods; and using locally reared and slow-cooked cheaper or, should I say, good-value, cuts of meat. I definitely belong to the second school. My "playground" days have long gone; now I want flavor and substance. And that's what slow cooking and the slow cooker deliver.

The slow cooker is the perfect tool for our economically straitened times, where the

restaurant customer or home cook demands ever better value for money. It perfectly uses the cheaper cuts at the front end of the animal, which require time for their best qualities to emerge. The slow cooker delivers "natural" food, as it's meant to be, with the flavors locked in. This it combines with a beautiful tenderness and such gentle cooking that the ingredients won't break up. Use it for a classic stew, delicate fish, custards, terrines, even warming punches; the slow cooker gives you so much versatility and scope.

I must own up to an initial nervousness when I started my slow cooker induction. Of course, I had cooked dishes long and slow before, on the stovetop and in the oven, and I was dubious about a kit that claimed to do it all for me. I was soon converted. The slow cooker's pluses are enormous: it uses less energy than a lightbulb; you can walk away knowing that your food won't burn or deteriorate even if you get home a little later than planned, and there are no cooking smells. It is one-pot dining at its best.

It's not magic though; there is still preparation to be done, but there are very few dishes to do at the end, which can't be a bad thing. The slow cooker has been around since the 1970s, but it never really took off until a couple of years ago. Most importantly, you can have great fun with it—use this book as a guide and add or subtract ingredients as you wish. As I found out, the key is to follow a few simple rules. For example, you can take one chicken recipe in this book and create another following the same cooking times.

High on the list is getting to know your machine—times and temperatures can vary and some models need preheating. It's also important to choose a machine that will suit the size of your family or personal needs. As a rough guide, for two you need at least a 2-quart machine, for four a 4-quart slow cooker, and for six or more a 5–8-quart slow cooker is essential. The recipes in this book generally use a 4-quart or 5-quart slow cooker. But as a general rule, buy a slow cooker that is bigger than your immediate needs because it's a great time-saver to make larger quantities and freeze the leftovers. A good tip is to freeze the food in the slow cooker's ceramic pot, then tip out and bag the solid block—it can be returned to the pot like this for defrosting and reheating.

Most modern slow cookers have a removable pot, which makes it easy to bring the food directly to the table—and helps reduce dishwashing. The slight downside is that most pots are not dishwasher-proof, as the bases are often porous and absorb water; the pot might then crack when heated. I suggest an oval-shaped slow cooker, as it accommodates loaf pans, terrines, or custard-dishes better.

So enjoy your slow cooker. I've had great fun with it as a chef, and you will too. It's an essential kitchen gadget that will give you hours of use, destress your life, eliminate that last-minute rush to feed the family, and save you money while producing delicious food. I've outlined overleaf some rules that I learned as I became familiar with my slow cooker.

Antony Worrall Thompson

SLOW COOKER TIPS—ALL YOU NEED TO KNOW

Choosing your slow cooker

- Shape: an oval slow cooker is best. It is the most adaptable shape.
- Make sure your slow cooker has a glass lid: it enables you to monitor the cooking.
- Check the cooker's settings: most have low and high, but I would choose one that also has medium, warm, and auto settings for greater flexibility.
- Size: the recipes in this book use a 4-quart or 5-quart total capacity cooker, suitable for 4–8 people. If there are only two of you, consider freezing the extra.

Preheating your slow cooker

- Some cookers require preheating—check the manufacturer's instructions and, if necessary, preheat your cooker before you start a recipe.
- I never preheat an empty ceramic dish; just add a little liquid first. Most slow cookers will usually take an hour to heat up, but this can be shortened by adding boiling liquid.

Cooking times and temperatures

- Always read the manufacturer's instructions carefully: times and temperatures vary from model to model.
- Dishes usually take twice as long to cook on the low setting compared with the high setting. But where recipes in this book state that a dish should be cooked on low, it is important to follow that instruction for a succulent and tender result. The following table can act as a guide for cooking times.

Oven or stovetop	Low setting	High setting
15–30 minutes	4–6 hours	1½–2½ hours
30–60 minutes	6–8 hours	3–4 hours
1–5 hours	8–12 hours	4–6 hours

- The low setting: this suits meat and vegetable casseroles, chops, chicken pieces, braises, soups, custard-based puddings, rice, and fish.
- The high setting: this suits steamed foods and puddings, dishes that include a raising agent, patés or terrines, whole chickens, and whole joints of meat.
- Remember that the timings are for advice only: a dish will not spoil if left on for longer.
- When using your slow cooker for the first few times, make notes to identify correct cooking times (you may need to decrease or increase the times). Do this by squeezing or cutting the meat with a spoon to see whether it is fully cooked and tender. Likewise, be prepared to vary the quantity of liquid used.

Preparing ingredients

- Cut both meat and vegetables to the same size for even cooking.
- For most dishes, press solids below the liquid before cooking.
- Brown meat and vegetables for a better taste. Do this on the stove, in the traditional way, before adding to your slow cooker.
- Root vegetables can take longer to cook than most cuts of meat, so arrange the vegetables around the edge and up the side of the slow cooker, where the heating elements are located.

- Soak most legumes in cold water overnight, then boil on the stove for 10 minutes before adding to the slow cooker. Pearl barley, red, Puy, or green lentils don't need to be soaked.
- Add shellfish in the last 40–60 minutes.
- Do not fill the slow cooker completely: allow a gap of at least 1½in between the food and the top. However, make sure the slow cooker is at least half full, because the heating elements are arranged around the side.
- Some vegetables don't benefit from slow cooking: these include green crisp vegetables and Asian vegetables.
- Always use good stocks where possible. The slow cooker will produce excellent stock (see pages 218–219), which can be frozen.

Pasta, rice, and noodles
- Cook pasta in the traditional way to *al dente* before putting it into the slow cooker: add it in the last 15 minutes of the cooking time. Pasta turns soft if cooked from scratch in a slow cooker.
- For best results, use easy-cook rice: if you are using traditional rice such as basmati, rinse until the water is clear, to stop it from sticking. As a general rule, use 1 cup liquid for each ½ cup of rice.
- Noodles do not cook well in a slow cooker.

Cooking
- Avoid lifting the lid during cooking: the condensation produces a sealed environment that, if broken, will add another 20 minutes to the cooking time.
- There is little or no evaporation so, unless the setting is on high with the lid off, you will not have to add more water. A slow cooker recipe will generally need only half the liquid content of a traditional recipe.
- You should rarely have to stir to prevent burning and sticking, but you can stir toward the end of the cooking time when on high.
- Some puddings or sauces that have a base of milk and/or cream do not cook well in a slow cooker.

Toward the end of the cooking time
- If there is too much juice at the end, turn the slow cooker to high, remove the lid, and allow the excess liquid to evaporate.
- To thicken the cooking juices, fold in the cornstarch paste (made following the package instructions) 40–60 minutes before the end of the cooking time. If you prefer to make a roux-based thickener, add the flour when browning the meat or vegetables.
- Always taste the dish at the end to check seasoning: flavors develop during cooking and it may not need as much as you think.

Safety
- The outside casing of most slow cookers gets hot, so use oven mitts.

Caring for your slow cooker
- Do not soak the ceramic pot in water to clean it: the base is usually porous, and any absorbed water could cause it to crack when next heated.
- Never put the hot ceramic pot on a cold surface, into cold water, or on the stove—it could crack.
- The glaze on the ceramic dish may develop a network of fine cracks after a few months: this does not affect how the cooker works.

Soups
&
sauces

Pea and ham soup

see page 30

Roasted yellow pepper soup **16**

Red lentil and white bean soup
with crisp pancetta **18**

Cauliflower and potato spice soup **19**

Baked onion soup with a Gruyère
cheese bread crust **20**

Celeriac vichyssoise **22**

Roast butternut and winter vegetable soup **24**

Chinese chicken "cure a cold" soup **25**

Seafood laksa **26**

Garbure **28**

Pea and ham soup **30**

A really useful Bolognese sauce **32**

SERVES **4** PREP **25** MINS COOKING **6–7** HRS SETTING **LOW**

Bell peppers deserve more in life than just ending up as an afterthought in a salad or as a crudité dipper for a healthy option. Here's a "real" bowl of soup to make the most of peppers in season.

Roasted yellow pepper soup

4 large yellow peppers, cored, seeded, and cut into 4 lengthways

3 tbsp olive oil

2½ tbsp butter

1 onion, finely chopped

1 garlic clove, finely chopped

1 small red chile, seeded and finely chopped

1 medium-sized potato, cut into ½in dice

1 oregano sprig

3 cups chicken or vegetable stock

salt and freshly ground black pepper

To garnish

croutons

grated Parmesan cheese

1. Place the pepper quarters, skin-side up, on the base of the broiler rack and drizzle with the oil. Cook under a hot broiler for 8–10 minutes until the peppers are softened and the skins have blackened in places.

2. Transfer the peppers to a plastic bag. Seal the end and allow the peppers to steam in their own heat for about 10 minutes. Peel off the skin. (Using a bag makes skinning the peppers less daunting and fiddly.)

3. Meanwhile, heat the butter in a skillet over low heat. Add the onion, garlic, and chile and sweat for 10 minutes or until softened but not browned.

4. Slice the peppers and add to the skillet with any broiling juices, the diced potato, oregano, stock, and seasoning. Bring to a boil, stirring, then pour into the slow cooker.

5. Cover and cook on low for 6–7 hours. Purée the soup in a blender until smooth and check the seasoning.

6. Ladle into bowls and serve with croutons and a little grated Parmesan.

A fiery topping
For a fiery topping to this soup, grill 6 large red chiles and 3 garlic cloves with a drizzle of olive oil until the garlic is golden and the chiles have blistered and charred. Peel, core, and seed the chiles, then blend in a pestle and mortar with the garlic, 2 tbsp balsamic vinegar, a pinch each of grated nutmeg and ground cumin and coriander, 1 tsp thyme leaves and 1 tsp oregano leaves. Season and spoon into a small jar with a lid. This will keep in the fridge for a couple of weeks. Stir into a little crème fraîche or sour cream to suit your fiery or not-so-fiery palate.

SERVES
4

PREP
15 MINS

COOKING
7–8 HRS

SETTING
LOW

If you're into your GI diet, as I am, this is the ideal soup as long as you keep it chunky. It has lovely deep flavors with the crisp pancetta (Italian bacon) being the perfect partner to the earthy tastes of the lentils and beans.

Red lentil and white bean soup with crisp pancetta

3 tbsp olive oil

3oz pancetta pieces

6 thyme sprigs

2 onions, finely chopped

4 garlic cloves, crushed to a paste with a little sea salt

1 red chile, finely chopped

1 heaping cup red lentils, rinsed and drained

14oz can chopped tomatoes

2½ pints vegetable stock

2 x 14oz cans cannellini beans, rinsed and drained

4 slices of pancetta

salt and freshly ground black pepper

1. Heat the oil in a skillet, add the pancetta pieces, and cook over medium heat until starting to crisp. Add the thyme, onions, garlic, and chile and cook for 8 minutes over low heat, to soften but not color.

2. Pour this mixture into the slow cooker, then add all the remaining ingredients except the pancetta slices to the slow cooker. Cover and cook on low for 7–8 hours. Check the seasoning before serving.

3. Meanwhile, in a dry nonstick skillet, cook the pancetta slices over medium heat until the fats have been released and the pancetta is crisp (the pancetta will continue to crisp up after it's been removed from the pan and dried on a rack).

4. The soup can be blitzed for a smooth texture, but I prefer to serve it chunky, topped with a slice of crisp pancetta.

A vegetarian alternative
For a vegetarian soup, just omit the pancetta and serve with some deep-fried, thinly sliced eggplant.

SERVES
4

PREP
15 MINS

COOKING
6–8 HRS

SETTING
LOW

It's amazing that you don't see more recipes for cauliflower soup because it has such a velvety finish and, with the addition of these wonderful spices, it becomes a lovely dish for your soup library.

Cauliflower and potato spice soup

2 medium-sized onions, thinly sliced

4 garlic cloves, finely chopped

6 tbsp unsalted butter

2 red chiles, finely sliced

1 tsp coriander seeds

pinch of yellow mustard seeds

pinch of fenugreek seeds (optional)

½ tsp cumin seeds

½ tsp freshly ground black pepper

1 tsp ground turmeric

1 tsp sweet paprika

1 tsp grated fresh ginger

1 medium-sized potato, diced

1½ cups desiccated coconut, soaked in 1¼ cups warm water for 15 minutes

3½ cups vegetable stock

1 large cauliflower, cut into small florets

14fl oz can coconut milk

1¼ cups heavy cream

salt

to garnish
cilantro leaves

1. In a skillet over medium heat, cook the onions and garlic gently in the butter for 6–8 minutes or until the onion has softened but not colored.

2. Add the chiles, coriander seeds, mustard seeds, fenugreek seeds, cumin, if using, black pepper, turmeric, paprika, and ginger and cook for 1 minute, then stir to combine. Transfer this mixture to your slow cooker.

3. Add the potatoes, the coconut and its soaking water, and the stock. Add the cauliflower and coconut milk, cover, and cook on a low setting for 6–8 hours.

4. Ladle the soup into a liquidizer and blend until smooth. Pass through a fine sieve and return to the slow cooker. If too thick, thin with extra stock. Add the cream, turn the slow cooker to high, and cook, uncovered, for a further 20 minutes.

5. Season to taste with salt and garnish with cilantro leaves.

Slow cooker tips
If you have an immersion hand blender, purée the soup while it is still in the slow cooker; it's quick, easy, and means fewer dishes to wash. If not, transfer the soup in batches to a liquidizer or food processor and blend until smooth, then pour back into the slow cooker to keep hot.

SERVES 4 | PREP 20 MINS | COOKING 1½ HRS | STOVE & OVEN

You can't beat a good bowl of onion soup, but onions need long slow cooking to get that beautiful sweetness.

Baked onion soup with a Gruyère cheese bread crust

6 tbsp unsalted butter

1 tbsp olive oil

2¼lb Spanish onions, finely sliced

1 garlic clove, finely chopped

1 tsp soft thyme leaves

1 bay leaf

salt and freshly ground black pepper

⅔ cup red wine

2 pints beef stock

1 tsp superfine sugar

8 x 1in slices of toasted baguette or French stick

1½ cups Gruyère cheese, grated

1. Heat 4 tablespoons of the butter and the oil in a large, heavy-based skillet, add the onions, garlic, thyme, and bay leaf, cover with wet parchment paper and a lid, and cook over very low heat for 1 hour, until the onions have turned golden and are meltingly soft. During the cooking, stir the onions from time to time, to stop them from burning. Season to taste.

2. Add the wine, stock, and sugar, then bring to a boil and simmer for 15 minutes.

3. Preheat the oven to 400°F.

4. If the skillet is ovenproof (if not, transfer to an earthenware soup tureen), place the bread slices on top, sprinkle with Gruyère cheese, and then drizzle the remaining butter, melted, over the cheese. Bake in a hot oven for 15 minutes or until bubbling and golden.

To make this in a slow cooker

Heat the butter and oil in a large, heavy-based skillet, add the onions, garlic, thyme, and bay leaf and cook over medium heat for 10–12 minutes, until the onions have started to soften and color. Transfer to your slow cooker, cover with wet parchment paper and a lid, and cook on low for 5–6 hours. Turn the slow cooker to high and cook, uncovered, for 20 minutes to darken the onions, stirring from time to time. Add the wine, stock, sugar, and seasoning, cover, and cook for 40 minutes. Then continue with step 4 above.

SERVES
4

PREP
25 MINS

COOKING
6¼–7¼ HRS

SETTING
LOW

What do you do with the knobbliest of vegetables, the celeriac? I'm a fan of mashed celeriac, but I'm also over the moon that it makes a really interesting soup.

Celeriac vichyssoise

2 tbsp vegetable oil

1 onion, finely chopped

1 tsp soft thyme leaves

1 bay leaf

1 garlic clove, finely chopped

1 celeriac, (approximately 1lb), cut into ½in dice

1 medium-sized potato, cut into ½in dice

1 tbsp lemon juice

3¼ cups chicken or vegetable stock

salt and freshly ground black pepper

⅔ cup milk

1¼ cups heavy cream

to garnish

few chopped chives or tiny celery leaves

1. Heat the oil in a large pan over medium heat. Add the onion, thyme, bay leaf, and garlic and sweat for about 10 minutes until softened but not browned.

2. Add the celeriac, potato, and lemon juice, then mix in the stock and seasoning. Bring to a boil, stirring, then transfer to the slow cooker pot.

3. Crumple up a large piece of wet parchment paper and press just beneath the surface of the stock to keep the vegetables submerged. Cover and cook on low for 6–7 hours, until the vegetables are tender. Remove the paper.

4. Purée the soup until smooth using an immersion hand blender or transfer in batches to a blender and then return it to the slow cooker pot. Stir in the milk and half the cream. Cover and heat for 15 minutes, then ladle into bowls.

5. Swirl the remaining cream over the top and garnish with chives or tiny celery leaves and a little more freshly ground black pepper.

MAKE THIS SOUP CHILLED
In the summertime this soup is delicious served chilled and garnished with ice cubes.

Slow cooker tips
Celeriac can turn brown, so don't forget to add the lemon juice and keep the vegetables submerged in the liquid by adding a layer of crumpled wet parchment paper.

SERVES **4–6** PREP **50** MINS COOKING **5½** HRS SETTING **LOW & HIGH**

**Squash and beans make a surprisingly good partnership—a lovely
winter warmer.**

Roast butternut and winter vegetable soup

2 butternut squash, peeled, seeded,
and cut into wedges

2 onions, roughly chopped

2 carrots, roughly chopped

2 celery stalks, cut into
(½in) dice

2 tbsp good olive oil

6 garlic cloves

1 tbsp finely chopped sage

3 pints vegetable stock

2 x 14oz cans cannellini, navy,
or great Northern beans,
rinsed and drained

salt and freshly ground black pepper

for the parsley purée

2 garlic cloves, roughly chopped

1 tsp sea salt

1 bunch flat-leaf parsley, finely chopped

4 tbsp freshly grated Parmesan

4 tbsp good olive oil

juice of ½ lemon

1. Preheat the oven to 350ºF.

2. Place the squash and the other vegetables with the olive oil in a roasting
pan and roast in the oven for about 45 minutes or until the squash has
softened and caramelized. Transfer to your slow cooker.

3. Add the garlic and sage with the stock and half the beans, cover, and
cook on low for 5 hours.

4. Place the soup in a liquidizer and blend until smooth. Return to the slow
cooker, add the remaining beans, and turn to high. Cover and cook for
20 minutes. Season to taste.

5. For the parsley purée: blend the garlic, sea salt, parsley, and Parmesan
in a food processor and drizzle in the olive oil until smooth. Add lemon
juice to taste.

6. Serve with 1 tsp parsley purée in each bowl of hot soup.

Also try
The parsley purée will keep for 3 days in the fridge. It's also good as a dip
or folded into pasta for a quick supper.

SERVES
4

PREP
20 MINS

COOKING
4¼ HRS

SETTING
LOW &
HIGH

It is always said that a Jewish mom would soothe any family ailment with a bowl of chicken soup that's "guaranteed to cure anything." I'm not so sure about that, but chicken soup definitely makes you feel better, and with chiles to add the sweat factor, maybe this will actually cure your cold!

Chinese chicken "cure a cold" soup

6oz skinless, boneless chicken thighs, cut into thin strips

1 tsp grated fresh ginger

½ lemongrass stalk, tough outer leaves removed, very finely chopped

2 kaffir lime leaves, fresh or dried

2 tsp red curry paste

2 garlic cloves, finely sliced

2 red chiles, finely diced

8 whole baby corn, halved lengthways

1 carrot, finely sliced

3½ pints good chicken stock, nearly boiling

4 scallions, finely sliced on the diagonal

8 small shiitake mushrooms, stalks removed, finely sliced

1 heaping cup snow peas, trimmed

1 cup small broccoli florets or thinly sliced stalks

2 tbsp soy sauce

1 tbsp lime juice

salt and freshly ground black pepper

1. Place the first 10 ingredients into your slow cooker, cover and cook on low for 4 hours.

2. Increase the setting to high, add the scallions, mushrooms, snow peas, and broccoli and cook, uncovered, for 15 minutes. Finally, pour in the soy and lime juice, check the seasoning and serve piping hot.

Bulk up
To bulk up the soup a little more, pour boiling water over 6oz rice noodles. Leave to soak for 3 minutes, drain, and add to the bowls before pouring over the soup.

SERVES
4

PREP
20 MINS

COOKING
3¼–4¼ HRS

SETTING
LOW & HIGH

Good "bowl food" is always a treat and in this dish you have some lovely flavors with a little kick. Monkfish is the perfect fish for the slow cooker because it stays intact.

Seafood laksa

peanut oil, for cooking

8 small squid, cleaned and cut into 2in pieces

1lb monkfish fillet, skinned and cut into 2in chunks

juice of 1 large lemon

2 medium-hot red chiles, halved and seeded

4 garlic cloves, roughly chopped

2in piece of fresh ginger, roughly chopped

1 tsp ground toasted coriander seeds

small bunch cilantro (including roots)

¼ cup sesame oil

2½ cups coconut milk

2 cups fish or vegetable stock

12 raw jumbo shrimp, peeled and deveined

3 cups snow peas, trimmed

2 bok choy, halved

7oz dried vermicelli

¼ cup Thai fish sauce (nam pla)

handful mint and basil leaves

3 scallions, thinly sliced

1. Heat a grill pan to very hot, brush with a little peanut oil, and then cook the squid for 30–45 seconds on each side until golden. Place on a plate and leave to cool.

2. Add the monkfish to the grill pan and brown all over. Squeeze over the lemon juice and set aside with the squid.

3. Heat a large skillet. Place the chiles in a food processor with the garlic, ginger, ground coriander seeds, fresh cilantro, and sesame oil, then blend to a coarse paste. Add this laksa paste to the heated skillet and stir-fry for 1 minute, then pour in the coconut milk and stock and bring to a boil. Spoon into your slow cooker with the squid and the monkfish, then cover and cook on low for 3–4 hours.

4. Add the shrimp, snow peas, and bok choy, and cook, uncovered, on high for 15 minutes.

5. Meanwhile, place the vermicelli in a large pan of boiling salted water and then immediately remove from the heat. Set aside for 3–4 minutes, depending on the manufacturer's instructions, then drain and refresh under cold running water. Set aside.

6. Add the fish sauce to the slow cooker pot with half the herbs and stir gently for a few seconds.

7. Divide the cooked vermicelli between the serving bowls and ladle the seafood laksa on top, then sprinkle over the remaining mint and basil leaves and the scallions. Serve piping hot.

Also try
Why not try octopus instead of squid, and scallops or crab instead of shrimp?

SERVES
6–8

PREP
20 MINS

SOAK
OVER-
NIGHT

COOKING
3¾ HRS

STOVE

Nothing is nicer than a bowl of this southwestern French dish on a cold day. Don't try to hurry this. The secret is in the long slow cooking until the meat is quite literally falling off the hock bone and the flavors have blended together.

Garbure

1¼ cups navy beans or great Northern beans, soaked overnight in cold water

8oz piece of salt pork

2 medium leeks, shredded

½lb new potatoes, washed and halved

6 celery stalks, thinly sliced

6 baby turnips

1 cured ham soaked overnight in cold water

6 garlic cloves, finely chopped

2 thyme sprigs

2 onions, thinly sliced

2 carrots, thinly sliced

2 bay leaves

1½ quarts chicken stock

1 small Savoy cabbage, shredded

4 duck confit legs, meat shredded

salt and freshly ground black pepper

to garnish
roughly chopped flat-leaf parsley

1. Drain the beans and boil in unsalted water for 40 minutes. Drain and discard the cooking water. Put the beans into a large saucepan and add the pork, leeks, potatoes, celery, turnips, ham, garlic, thyme, onions, carrots, bay leaves, and stock. Simmer for 2 hours 45 minutes, skimming off the scum from time to time, until the meat is cooked through.

2. Add the cabbage and duck confit, and simmer for a further 20 minutes.

3. Remove the salt pork and ham. Place the salt pork in a food processor and blend until smooth, then stir it back into the soup. Remove the meat from the ham and shred, then fold into the soup. Season to taste and garnish with parsley.

SERVES
4

PREP
15 MINS

SOAK
OVER-
NIGHT

COOKING
8 HRS

SETTING
LOW

We've grown used to making pea soup with frozen peas—nothing wrong with that—but for real flavor, the slow cooker comes into its own with the genuine article, split peas.

Pea and ham soup

¾lb split green peas

1 tbsp canola oil

1 onion, finely chopped

4 garlic cloves, finely chopped

1 tsp soft thyme leaves

2 bay leaves

2¼lb cured ham, soaked overnight in cold water

2 medium carrots, finely diced

2 celery stalks, finely diced

3¾ pints chicken stock

salt and freshly ground black pepper

to garnish

½ cup plain, strained yogurt

2 tsp very finely chopped mint

2 tsp very finely chopped chives

1. Rinse the peas under cold water and drain.

2. In a skillet, heat the oil over medium heat and gently cook the onion, garlic, thyme, and bay for 10 minutes, until the onion has softened but has not colored. Spoon into your slow cooker.

3. Add all the remaining soup ingredients, except the seasoning, to the slow cooker, then cover and cook on low heat for 8 hours, until the meat is cooked through.

4. Remove the ham from the cooker. Allow to cool enough to handle, then cut off and discard the rind and most of the fat. Remove the meat from the bone and coarsely chop, then stir it back into the soup. Season to taste.

5. For the garnish, combine all the ingredients. Spoon a dollop on top of each bowl of soup and gring over some black pepper.

SERVES
12

PREP
30 MINS

COOKING
10½ HRS
LARGE POT

SETTING
LOW & HIGH

Over the past decade, dishes using ground beef have fallen from favor with many people, which is a pity. This Bolognese sauce is a perfect standby for converting into any type of ground-beef dish, such as moussaka, cannelloni, chili con carne, lasagne, and fillings for meat pies and baked potatoes. It's an ideal recipe to make in big batches for the freezer.

A really useful Bolognese sauce

4oz smoked bacon or pancetta, diced

up to 1¼ cups good olive oil

2 onions, finely diced

2 celery stalks, finely diced

2 carrots, finely sliced

5 garlic cloves, crushed to a paste with
   a little sea salt

2 bay leaves

2 tsp dried oregano

4lb ground beef

2 x 14oz cans chopped tomatoes

2 tbsp tomato paste

1 tbsp anchovy essence

2 tbsp Worcestershire sauce

9oz fresh chicken livers, finely chopped

1 bottle red wine

2 pints chicken, beef, or lamb stock

2 tbsp basil leaves

1 tbsp fresh oregano leaves

salt and freshly ground black pepper

1. In a large skillet, fry the bacon in 1 tbsp olive oil over medium heat. When the bacon is crisp and has released some fat, add the onions, celery, carrots, garlic, bay leaves, and dried oregano and cook until the vegetables have softened and taken on a little color. Spoon into the slow cooker.

2. Then in the same skillet, heat 1 tbsp olive oil and fry the ground beef over high heat in small batches until browned. While the meat is frying, break up any lumps with the back of a wooden spoon. When browned, add the meat to the vegetable mix in the slow cooker.

3. Add the canned tomatoes, tomato paste, anchovy essence, Worcestershire sauce, chicken livers, red wine, and stock and stir. Cover and cook on low for 10 hours until the meat is cooked. Stir to combine.

4. Turn the cooker to high and stir in the herbs, season to taste, then cook, uncovered, for 20 minutes.

On the side

Apricot and orange chutney

see page 48

Aromatic eggplant with feta and spinach **38**

Rice with some nice spice **40**

Slow-cooked zucchini **41**

Slow-cooked fennel with tomatoes,
olives, and crispy crumbs **42**

Red lentil dip **44**

Spicy braised eggplant with prunes **45**

Prosciutto-wrapped braised celery **46**

Apricot and orange chutney **48**

Love them or hate them, eggplants are very much part of our supermarket shelves, but they do need added flavor. This is a dip-cum-vegetable starter with loads going on and a great taste.

Aromatic eggplant with feta and spinach

2¼lb eggplant

3 tbsp peanut oil

2 tbsp finely chopped garlic

1 tbsp grated fresh ginger

8 scallions, finely sliced

¾ tsp dried red pepper flakes

5 tbsp light soy sauce

4 tbsp soft dark brown sugar

1 tbsp rice vinegar

2 tbsp mirin or dry sherry

6oz good feta cheese, diced

1 tsp sesame oil

¾lb baby spinach

1 tbsp roughly chopped cilantro leaves

4 tbsp plain, strained yogurt (optional)

1. Place the eggplant directly over the gas flame on your stove or under a very hot broiler and cook until charred all over, turning from time to time (this gives a much smokier flavor).

2. When cool enough to handle, scrape off the charred skin and roughly chop the flesh. Add to your slow cooker.

3. Meanwhile, put the peanut oil in a wok or skillet over high heat, then add the garlic, ginger, scallions, and dried red pepper flakes and stir-fry for 30 seconds. Add the soy sauce, sugar, rice vinegar, and mirin or dry sherry and stir to combine. Cook for 1 minute.

4. Fold into the eggplant in the slow cooker, cover, and cook on low for 5–6 hours. Then turn your cooker to high and fold in the feta, sesame oil, spinach, and chopped cilantro. Cook, uncovered, for 15 minutes.

5. Serve with a dollop of yogurt if you like.

SERVING SUGGESTION
Serve with raw vegetable crudités, or with long-grain rice, noodles, or pitta bread.

SERVES
4

PREP
25 MINS

COOKING
3 HRS

SETTING
LOW &
HIGH

Some of my favorite meals involve a bowl of rice with loads of bits and pieces. I'm a recent convert to brown rice, having found out that white rice has been stripped of most of its goodness. This dish could act as a base for all sorts of other goodies—shrimp, pork, chicken, leftovers from the Sunday roast—and it's equally delicious as a vegetarian dish.

Rice with some nice spice

2 tbsp sunflower or vegetable oil

1 onion, finely chopped

3 garlic cloves, crushed to a paste with a little sea salt

1 carrot, finely diced

1 celery stick, finely sliced

1⅓ cups easy-cook brown rice, rinsed and drained

½ tsp each garam masala, chili powder and ground cumin, coriander, and turmeric

2½ cups vegetable stock, boiling

8oz can chopped tomatoes

8oz can corn, drained

2 roasted peppers, from a jar, cut into small dice

2 handfuls baby spinach

2 tbsp unsalted butter

salt and freshly ground black pepper

3 tbsp cashews, roughly chopped

1. Heat the oil in a skillet, then add the onion, garlic, carrot, and celery and cook gently for 10 minutes, until the vegetables have started to soften but haven't taken on much color.

2. Add the rice and spices and cook for 2 minutes, stirring constantly, then transfer the contents of the skillet into your slow cooker. Pour in the stock, tomatoes, and corn, cover, and cook on low for 2 hours.

3. Lift the lid, fold in the peppers, then lay the spinach on the surface and dot with the butter. Increase the setting to high, cover, and cook for 40 minutes.

4. Stir in the spinach (which will have collapsed), season to taste, and scatter with cashews.

SERVING SUGGESTION
You could serve this with a salad, a bowl of dhal (see page 161), or a dollop of your favorite raita.

SERVES
6

PREP
10 MINS

COOKING
3–5 HRS

SETTING
LOW &
HIGH

Going against all zucchini cooking principles, this most unattractive of dishes has beautiful flavors. After all, beauty is more than skin deep— I should know! Serve as a warm vegetable or at room temperature as part of a meze buffet.

Slow-cooked zucchini

4 tbsp extra-virgin olive oil

3 garlic cloves, finely chopped

2–3 dried chiles, crumbled

1½lb mixed green and yellow zucchini, roughly chopped into 1in chunks

grated zest of 2 unwaxed or organic lemons and juice of ½ lemon

salt and freshly ground black pepper

2 tbsp roughly chopped flat-leaf parsley

3 tbsp finely chopped mint

1. Heat half the olive oil in a large heavy-based skillet, add the garlic and chile, and cook over low heat for 2–3 minutes, stirring from time to time; the garlic should be a golden color. Transfer to your slow cooker.

2. Stir in the zucchini and lemon zest and season with salt and pepper. Cover and cook for 3–5 hours on low. The zucchini will gradually collapse, and become very soft.

3. Turn the heat to high and fold in the parsley, mint, and lemon juice. Drizzle with the remaining olive oil. Cook, uncovered, for 10 minutes. This dish can be eaten either hot or at room temperature.

Also try
If you grow your own zucchini, the flowers are delicious to eat; try them dipped in batter and deep-fried or stuffed, dipped in batter, and then deep-fried.

If you think you don't like fennel, think again. Here the fennel loses its aggression, mellows into blissful harmony with the other ingredients, and then you're smacked in the mouth with glorious crunchy crumbs.

Slow-cooked fennel with tomatoes, olives, and crispy crumbs

4 fennel bulbs, tough outer layer removed

¾ cup extra-virgin olive oil

1 bulb of garlic, split into cloves and peeled

2 tbsp chopped soft oregano leaves

½ cup dry white wine

14oz can good-quality chopped tomatoes

salt and freshly ground black pepper

2 tbsp balsamic vinegar

24 Kalamata olives, pitted and roughly chopped

12 basil leaves, ripped

for the bread topping

2 garlic cloves

1 tbsp soft thyme leaves

2 tsp rosemary leaves

2 tbsp flat-leaf parsley leaves

⅔ cup good olive oil

2-day-old ciabatta loaf, broken into small pieces

1 tbsp pumpkin seeds

4 tbsp grated Parmesan

to serve

new potatoes or salad

1. Quarter the fennel lengthways, then place in a large skillet and cook in the olive oil over medium heat for 15 minutes, turning regularly until golden all over.

2. Add the garlic, oregano, wine, tomatoes, and ⅔ cup boiling water. Bring to a boil and transfer to your slow cooker. Cover and cook on low for 6–7 hours, then season with salt, black pepper, and balsamic vinegar. Fold in the olives and basil, then cook, uncovered, on high for 15 minutes.

3. Meanwhile, for the bread topping: finely chop together the garlic and herbs. Heat the olive oil in a skillet over medium heat, add the ciabatta pieces, and fry until golden. Fold in the remaining ingredients and stir to combine. Scatter over the slow-cooked fennel.

4. Serve this dish either hot or at room temperature with new potatoes or a leafy salad.

SERVES
4

PREP
15 MINS

COOKING
6–8 HRS

SETTING
LOW

A great dip for vegetarians and meat-eaters alike. If you thin the
dip with vegetable stock after puréeing, it makes a delicious soup.
And, of course, it's lovely as a vegetable accompaniment.

Red lentil dip

4 tbsp extra-virgin olive oil

4 garlic cloves, finely chopped

1 onion, finely chopped

1 tsp ground cumin

1 tsp ground coriander

1 tsp fennel seeds

½ tsp cayenne pepper

½lb split red lentils, rinsed
   and drained

2½ cups vegetable stock

2 tbsp sun-dried tomato pesto

1 tbsp lemon juice

salt and freshly ground black pepper

4 scallions, finely diced

2 tbsp finely chopped flat-leaf parsley

2 tbsp finely chopped cilantro

to serve

flat bread or raw vegetable crudités

1. Heat the olive oil in a pan, add the garlic and onion, and cook over
medium heat for 8 minutes, until the onion has softened but has not
colored. Add the spices and cook for a further 2 minutes. Transfer to your
slow cooker.

2. Add the lentils and stock, cover, and cook on low for 6–8 hours until the
lentils are tender, adding more hot stock if necessary.

3. Fold in the tomato pesto and lemon juice and beat with a heavy whisk or
wooden spoon until the lentils break up into a thick purée. (I like a textured
finish.) Season to taste and fold in the scallions, parsley, and cilantro.

4. Add more olive oil if the purée appears too dry, then serve with flat bread
or raw vegetable crudités.

SERVES
4

PREP
15 MINS

COOKING
3½–4½ HRS

SETTING
LOW & HIGH

Spicy braised eggplant with prunes

6 tbsp vegetable oil

1 tbsp sesame oil

2 large shiny eggplants, calyx removed, cut into 1in cubes

1 tbsp finely chopped garlic

1 tbsp grated fresh ginger

2 bunches scallions, cut into 1in batons

1¾ cups vegetable stock

2 tbsp soy sauce

¾ cup pitted prunes, chopped

1 tbsp salted Chinese black beans, finely chopped (optional)

1 tsp cornstarch, mixed to a paste with 2 tbsp water

to garnish

2 tbsp roughly chopped cilantro

1 green chile, seeded and finely diced

1. In a skillet, heat the oils and fry the eggplant over high heat for about 8 minutes, until brown all over. Place in the slow cooker.

2. Add the garlic, ginger, and scallions to the skillet and cook for 3 minutes, turning regularly. Combine with the eggplant, add the stock, soy sauce, prunes, and black beans, if using, cover, and cook on low for 3–4 hours.

3. Increase the heat to high and stir, then add the cornstarch paste, cover, and cook for 30 minutes to thicken.

4. Spoon the mixture into a dish and scatter with the cilantro and chile. Serve hot or at room temperature.

SERVING SUGGESTION
This is excellent as part of an Asian buffet. I serve it with scallion rice: fry a few sliced scallions for a couple of minutes in vegetable oil over medium heat, then stir in some cooked rice and fry briefly. Season with a splash of Thai fish sauce and garnish with roughly chopped cilantro.

SERVES
4

PREP
25 MINS

COOKING
6–8 HRS

SETTING
LOW

A classic recipe, which you don't see very often in cookbooks or, for that matter, in restaurants. It's delicious and spoon tender, and does wonders for what I believe is essentially a dull vegetable.

Prosciutto-wrapped braised celery

2 bunches of celery, trimmed

8 slices of prosciutto (Parma or Serrano ham)

4 tbsp unsalted butter

1 tbsp olive oil

1 onion, finely chopped

1 carrot, thinly sliced

2 garlic cloves, finely chopped

3½oz smoked bacon, cut into lardons

½ tsp soft thyme leaves

¾lb piece of pork rind (optional)

1 tsp anchovy essence

¼ cup dry red wine

2 cups strong chicken or beef stock

freshly ground black pepper

¼ grated Parmesan

1. Cut the leafy tops off each bunch of celery (retain for another use), leaving a 6in heart. Remove strings from the outside stalks. Plunge the celery hearts into boiling salted water and cook for 10 minutes. Drain and set aside to cool slightly, then cut the celery in half lengthways. Wrap each half in 2 slices of prosciutto.

2. Meanwhile, heat the butter and olive oil in a Dutch oven over medium heat. Add the onion, carrot, garlic, bacon, and thyme and cook for 8 minutes, stirring occasionally.

3. If using, place the pork rind, fat-side down, on the bottom of your slow cooker and place the celery hearts on top. Surround them with the vegetables and bacon. Add the anchovy essence, wine, and stock. Cover and cook on low for 6–8 hours. Season with pepper to taste.

4. Sprinkle with grated Parmesan and glaze under a hot broiler.

SERVING SUGGESTION
You could serve this as an appetizer or with roast or grilled meat.

Also try
This also works well with 2 bulbs of fennel.

MAKES
6 x 1lb JARS

PREP
15 MINS

COOKING
6–7 HRS

SETTING
LOW

One of my favorite chutneys and it's perfect for the slow cooker. It's superb with cold meats and cheese.

Apricot and orange chutney

4 organic oranges, unpeeled, chopped into ¾in pieces and seeds removed

3¼lb apricots, pitted and quartered

1lb onions, roughly diced

1lb superfine sugar

1 tsp sea salt

½ tsp cloves

1 tsp freshly ground black pepper

½ tsp dried red pepper flakes

½ tsp ground mace

1 tsp medium-hot curry powder

1 tbsp yellow mustard seeds

1 tsp ground turmeric

2 cups apple cider vinegar

1. Mix together all the ingredients and pour into the slow cooker. Cover and cook on low for 6–7 hours, stirring from time to time, especially near the end of the cooking time.

2. Sterilize 6 clean jam jars by preheating the oven to 250°F and placing the jars in the bottom of the oven for 30 minutes. Then place the jars on a tray, ladle the chutney into the jars, and seal each jar with a lid.

3. Store for at least a week before consuming. The chutney will keep for up to 6 months in a cool, dry place, but store in the fridge once opened.

SERVING SUGGESTION
This chutney is delicious with red Leicester cheese or sharp Cheddar.

Also try
This can also be made with 1¾lb dried apricots. Soak them in water for 1 hour, then quarter and cook for the same length of time in the slow cooker.

Roasts & braises

Pot-roast chicken

see page 58

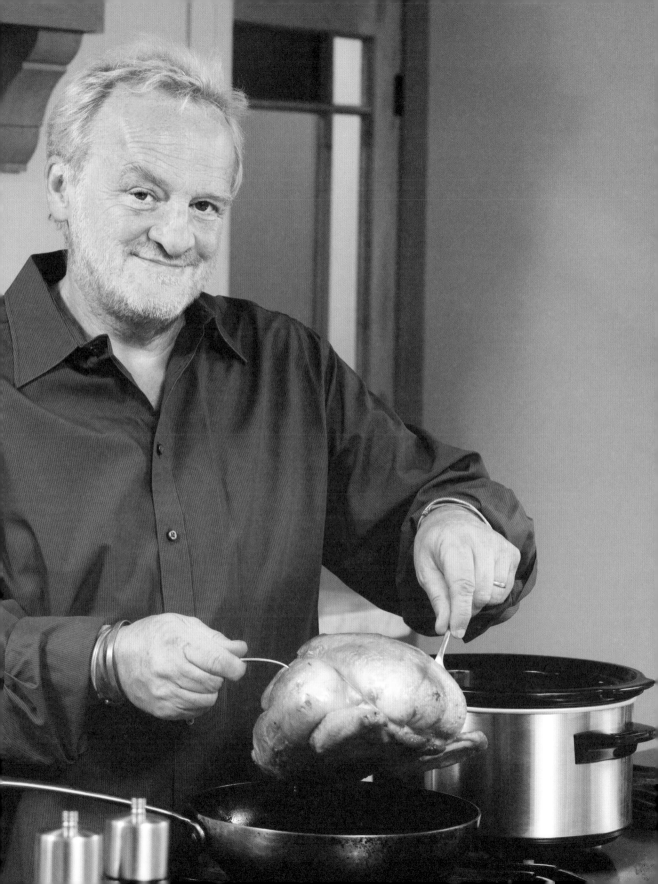

Braised squid with potatoes and peas **54**

Herby salmon fillets **56**

Jerk chicken **57**

Pot-roast chicken **58**

Moroccan spiced roast chicken **60**

Oven-roasted chicken with Med veg **62**

Aromatic chicken with oranges **64**

Spiced garlic and thyme roasted spatchcock chicken **66**

Italian poussin with white beans **68**

Pot-roasted partridge with hard cider and Calvados **70**

Braised pigeon with pine nuts and raisins **72**

Braised hare with Tolosa beans **74**

Braised sweetbreads with sorrel **75**

Spring lamb with vegetables **76**

Lamb steaks with rosemary garlic flageolet crust **78**

Arabian roast lamb and potatoes **80**

North African mutton with spiced fruits and nuts **82**

Braised calf's liver **83**

Pot-roasted beef with gremolata **84**

Braised beef with baby carrots and horseradish **86**

Pork fillets with prune and parsley stuffing **87**

Garlic and sage pork with fennel and pears **88**

Spicy pork in stout **90**

Poached pork shoulder **92**

Braised gammon and potatoes with a peach and
Barkham Blue cheese sauce **93**

Caramelized spareribs with bourbon and ginger **94**

SERVES
4

PREP
25 MINS

COOKING
4–6 HRS

SETTING
LOW

This is a beauty! The slow cooker was built with squid in mind: if you're not flash-frying or grilling it, you need a good thick stew packed with loads of flavor and memories of Mediterranean moments.

Braised squid with potatoes and peas

1lb potatoes, cut into ¾in dice

2 tbsp olive oil

1 onion, finely chopped

1¾lb squid, cleaned and
   squid tubes thickly sliced

4 garlic cloves, finely chopped

4 tbsp brandy

¾ cup dry white wine

14oz can chopped tomatoes

2 tsp tomato paste

1 thyme sprig

1 bay leaf

1 tsp smoked paprika

salt and freshly ground black pepper

1 cup shelled fresh peas, or
   frozen peas, defrosted

to garnish

roughly chopped flat-leaf parsley
   (optional)

to serve

torn chunks of crusty country bread

1. Add the potatoes to a saucepan of boiling water and parboil for 2–3 minutes. Drain.

2. Heat the oil in a large skillet, add the onion, and fry over medium heat, until just beginning to turn golden. Stir in the squid and garlic and cook for 2–3 minutes.

3. Warm the brandy in a small saucepan, ignite with a lit match, then carefully pour into the squid. When the flames subside, add the wine, tomatoes, tomato paste, herbs, paprika, and seasoning.

4. Bring to a boil, then transfer to the slow cooker pot. Cover and cook on low for 4–6 hours until the squid is tender.

5. Cook the peas in a pan of boiling water for 3 minutes just before you are ready to serve. Drain and stir into the squid.

6. Serve in shallow bowls sprinkled with a little chopped parsley, if you like, and torn bread to mop up the juices.

TO MAKE IT SPICIER
For chile fans, add 2 seeded, finely chopped fresh hot green chiles as well as the paprika.

Also try
You could also throw in some mussels and clams. Clean and discard any that do not close when tapped against the sink. For the last hour of cooking the braised squid, turn the slow cooker to high, add the shellfish, then cover and cook. Before serving, discard any mussels or clams that have not opened.

SERVES
4

PREP
15 MINS

MARINATE
30 MINS

COOKING
3–4 HRS

SETTING
LOW

Salmon is great fish for withstanding and accepting big flavors, and there are plenty of them in this dish. Keep the accompaniments simple—just a leafy salad and a few new potatoes will do.

Herby salmon fillets

4 x 6oz salmon fillets, skin on

1¼ cups fish or vegetable stock, hot

for the marinade

4 long mild fresh green chiles, roughly chopped

4 garlic cloves, roughly chopped

1 bunch cilantro, roughly chopped

1 bunch basil, roughly chopped

8 mint leaves

¾in piece of fresh ginger, roughly chopped

juice and grated zest of 2 unwaxed or organic lemons

4 tbsp canola or vegetable oil

to serve

fresh salad

boiled potatoes

1. For the marinade, place the chiles, garlic, half the cilantro, half the basil, the mint, ginger, lemon juice and zest, and oil in a blender or food processor and blend until smooth.

2. Pour the marinade over the salmon and rub well into the fish. Leave, covered, at room temperature for 30 minutes.

3. After 30 minutes place the salmon fillets, along with the marinade and the stock, into your slow cooker and cook on low for 3–4 hours.

4. At the end of the cooking time, fold the remaining cilantro and basil into the salmon. This will enhance the color of the dish—by the time it has finished cooking the herb paste will have turned to dull olive green and the addition of these herbs will revitalize the color.

5. Serve the salmon fillets with a simple salad and boiled potatoes.

SERVES
4

PREP
30 MINS

MARINATE
1 HR

COOKING
6–8 HRS

SETTING
LOW

I recently took part in a "jerk" (hot spice-rubbed meat) challenge on the beautiful island of Jamaica. I didn't win, but I did learn a thing or two, so I reckon my version is pretty authentic apart from the honey. I love the little bit of sweetness it adds, which contrasts perfectly with the fire of the chiles.

Jerk chicken

2 tbsp vegetable oil

12 boneless chicken thighs, skin and flesh slashed 3 times on each

2 onions, finely chopped

1 tbsp all-purpose flour

3 Scotch bonnet chiles

1 tbsp tomato paste

1¼ cups chicken stock

for the marinade

3 mild red chiles, roughly chopped

2 bunches scallions, roughly chopped

2 garlic cloves, roughly chopped

¼ tsp grated nutmeg

1in piece of fresh ginger, roughly chopped

½ tsp ground cinnamon

½ bunch thyme, roughly chopped

1 tbsp vegetable oil

1 tbsp clear honey

1 tbsp lime juice

1 tsp salt

freshly ground black pepper

to serve

home-made coleslaw, (see page 94)

long-grain rice

1. Put half the oil in a skillet over high heat and brown the chicken pieces all over. Set aside to cool.

2. Use a food processor or a mortar and pestle to make the marinade. Blitz or crush all the ingredients to a smooth paste. Transfer to a bowl.

3. Toss the browned chicken pieces in the marinade, cover with plastic wrap, and refrigerate for at least 1 hour, but preferably overnight.

4. Heat the remaining oil in a skillet and cook the onions over medium heat for 8–10 minutes, until softened and pale golden. Transfer to the slow cooker and sprinkle with the flour. Stir to combine, then add the Scotch bonnet chiles and tomato paste. Stir once again and add the stock, chicken, and marinade.

5. Cover and cook on low for 6–8 hours. Halfway through, check the taste of the sauce. Once it is hot and spicy enough to your liking, remove the Scotch bonnet chiles and discard, until the chicken is thoroughly cooked.

6. Serve with home-made apple coleslaw and rice.

SERVES
4

PREP
20 MINS

COOKING
7¼–8¼
HRS

SETTING
LOW &
HIGH

An all-time family favorite, which features at least once a month on my
household's domestic menu. Get the main structure of the pot-roast right
and your choice of vegetables can vary with the season.

Pot-roast chicken

1–2 tbsp olive oil

3¼lb free-range chicken

4oz smoked bacon, chopped

1 onion, roughly chopped

3 garlic cloves, finely chopped

2 celery stalks, cut into 1in chunks

2 carrots, cut into 1in chunks

12 baby new potatoes

1 tbsp soft thyme leaves

2 bay leaves

14oz can chopped tomatoes

1 tbsp Worcestershire sauce

3½ cups chicken or vegetable
stock, hot

3 cups broccoli florets

¾ cup frozen peas, defrosted

handful of spinach

¾ cup frozen baby fava beans,
defrosted

salt and freshly ground black pepper

1. Place a large skillet over high heat, add the olive oil and, when hot, add
the whole chicken to the pan, turning occasionally until brown all over.
Remove and place in your slow cooker.

2. Add the bacon to the skillet and fry for a few minutes over medium heat,
then add the onion, garlic, celery, carrots, potatoes, thyme, and bay leaves
and cook for a further 6 minutes.

3. Add the tomatoes and the Worcestershire sauce and bring to a boil.
Spoon into your slow cooker, add the stock, then cover and cook on low
for 7–8 hours until the chicken is cooked. To check if the chicken is cooked
through, push a skewer right into the thickest part of the thigh; if the juices
run clear it is cooked—any pink and it needs a bit longer.

4. Lift out the chicken onto a platter, cover with foil, and set aside in a
warm place to rest. Turn the slow cooker to high, stir the green vegetables
into the pot, and cook, uncovered, for 10 minutes until the vegetables are
tender. Season to taste.

5. Carve the chicken. Spoon the vegetables and broth into 4 warm bowls.

Also try
Use chicken thighs (bone in) instead of a whole chicken for a quicker
supper. Reduce the cooking time on low by half to 3½–4 hours.

SERVES
4

PREP
15 MINS

MARINATE
3½ HRS

COOKING
2 HRS

OVEN

If you'd like to add a little flavor to a rather tasteless chicken, this is the perfect recipe. I haven't found a better way of livening up a bland fowl.

Moroccan spiced roast chicken

3¼lb chicken

for the rub

1 bulb of garlic

2 tbsp olive oil

2 tbsp caraway seeds

1 tbsp cumin seeds

2 tsp ground turmeric

3 tsp dried rosemary

1½ tsp dried oregano

4 tbsp sea salt

½ bunch cilantro, roughly chopped

6 tbsp harissa paste

2 tsp superfine sugar

1 small onion, roughly chopped

2 tbsp plain, strained yogurt

freshly ground black pepper

to serve

couscous

leafy salad

1. Preheat the oven to 350°F.

2. Cut ½in off the top of the garlic bulb, drizzle a little of the oil over the cut surface, wrap in foil, and cook in the oven for 30 minutes. Allow to cool enough to handle, then unwrap, separate the garlic cloves, and squeeze the flesh from their papery wrapping. Set aside. Turn the oven off.

3. Grind all the dried spices, dried herbs, and salt in a mortar and pestle (or electric coffee grinder), then combine with the garlic and all the other ingredients for the rub, including the remaining oil, in a food processor and purée until smooth. (This will keep in the fridge for up to 2 weeks.)

4. Rub 2 tbsp of the rub over the skin and the cavity of the chicken, cover with plastic wrap, and refrigerate for at least 3 hours, but preferably overnight. Take the chicken out of the fridge and allow it to come to room temperature for at least 30 minutes. Meanwhile, preheat the oven to 350°F.

5. Roast the chicken for 1½ hours until the meat is cooked and the juices run clear when the thickest part of the thigh is pierced with a skewer, then allow to rest for 10 minutes before carving.

6. Serve with couscous and a leafy salad.

SERVES
4

PREP
20 MINS

COOKING
1½ HRS

OVEN

There's something special to be said for a dish that comes fully loaded so you don't need all kinds of pans, greatly reducing the amount of dishwashing that needs to be done. I've suggested some vegetables, but please feel free to mix and match.

Oven-roasted chicken with Med veg

3¼lb free-range chicken

⅔ cup good olive oil

salt and freshly ground black pepper

½ lemon

½ white onion, peeled

4 thyme sprigs

2 bay leaves

¾lb new or fingerling potatoes

1 small eggplant, calyx removed, cut into 1in dice

½ butternut squash, peeled, seeded, and cut into 1in dice

1 red onion, cut into quarters

1 fennel bulb, tough outer layer removed, quartered lengthways

2 zucchini, cut into 1in disks

12 garlic cloves, unpeeled

3 tbsp good balsamic vinegar

1 tbsp marjoram or oregano leaves

1. Preheat the oven to 400°F.

2. Rub the chicken all over with 2 tbsp olive oil and season with salt and pepper. Place the lemon, white onion, 1 thyme sprig, and the bay leaves inside the cavity of the chicken.

3. Place the chicken on a roasting pan with the potatoes and roast for 30 minutes. Add the eggplant, squash, red onion, and fennel and douse with the remaining olive oil, return to the oven, and cook for a further 30 minutes before adding the zucchini, garlic, and the remaining thyme. Toss with the other vegetables, season, and return to the oven for 30 minutes, basting and turning the vegetables regularly, until the chicken is cooked through and the juices run clear when the thickest part of the thigh is pierced with a skewer.

4. Remove the chicken to a warm platter, cover loosely with foil and keep warm while it rests.

5. Meanwhile, place the roasting pan with the vegetables on your stove over medium heat, add the balsamic vinegar and marjoram, and toss together with the roasting juices. Spoon the vegetables and juices around the chicken.

SERVES
4

PREP
15 MINS

COOKING
6½–8½
HRS

SETTING
LOW &
HIGH

A beautifully flavored chicken dish inspired by the rustic cuisine of Spain. You can also fold in some blanched fava beans and peas, if the mood grabs you, for the last 10 minutes of cooking.

Aromatic chicken with oranges

4 tbsp olive oil

4 chicken breasts, skin on

4 boneless chicken thighs, skin on

4 cloves

3 organic oranges, unpeeled and cut into 1in chunks

4 garlic cloves, crushed to a paste with a little sea salt

3oz pancetta, diced or lardons

4 thyme sprigs

1lb pickling onions or small shallots, peeled

1 unwaxed or organic lemon, cut into 1in chunks

1 tsp smoked paprika

¾ cup Manzanilla sherry

salt and freshly ground black pepper

to garnish

¼ cup flaked almonds, toasted

to serve

toasted chunks of country bread

garlic clove

new potatoes

1. Put the oil in a large skillet over medium heat, then fry the chicken breasts and thighs until brown all over. Transfer the chicken to your slow cooker using long-handled tongs.

2. Poke the cloves into the orange pieces.

3. Add the garlic, pancetta, thyme, onions, clove-studded orange pieces, and lemon to the skillet and fry for 5 minutes, until the onions are brown. Stir in the paprika.

4. Place this mixture in your slow cooker on top of the chicken. Add the sherry and 1¼ cups water, cover, and cook on low for 6–8 hours, until the chicken is thoroughly cooked.

5. Remove the chicken pieces with half the fruit and onions, and keep them warm.

6. Turn the slow cooker to high, and cook the remaining fruit and onions, uncovered, for 20 minutes. Then mash the sauce, roughly crushing the fruit and onions.

7. Return the chicken with the reserved fruit and onions to the slow cooker pot, season to taste, then cover and warm through on high for 10 minutes.

8. Spoon the sauce over the chicken and scatter over a few toasted flaked almonds. Serve with a toasted chunk of country bread, rubbed with a garlic clove, and new potatoes.

Also try
Try cooking this with rabbit pieces instead of chicken breasts and thighs. Use a similar quantity of meat and the same cooking times.

SERVES
4

PREP
20 MINS

COOKING
6 HRS

SETTING
LOW

When a chicken had been split down the length of its backbone and spread out flat it is known as a spatchcock. This recipe has a lovely balance of sweet and sour from the sugar and lemon.

Spiced garlic and thyme roasted spatchcock chicken

¼ cup extra-virgin olive oil

3¼lb free-range chicken, spatchcocked

1 tsp dried red pepper flakes

3 garlic cloves, crushed to a paste with a little sea salt

½ tsp smoked paprika

3 tsp dried thyme

grated zest and juice of 1 unwaxed or organic lemon

¼ cup sherry vinegar

2 tbsp dark muscovado sugar

½ tsp freshly ground black pepper

4 thyme sprigs

1 unwaxed or organic lemon, halved

1. Heat a little of the olive oil in a nonstick Dutch oven and brown the chicken on both sides over high heat, until golden. Place the chicken in the slow cooker. Mix all the remaining ingredients together, add to the chicken, and stir to combine.

2. Cover with the lid and cook on low for 6 hours or until the chicken is thoroughly cooked and the juices run clear when pierced with a skewer.

3. Lift out the chicken onto a warmed serving platter, cover with foil, and allow to rest for 15 minutes. Drizzle with any cooking juices and serve.

SERVING SUGGESTION
This is lovely in the summer with a salad or in the winter with roasted vegetables and mashed potatoes.

How to spatchcock a chicken
To spatchcock: split the chicken lengthways down the length of the backbone with a knife or poultry shears and remove the backbone and small rib bones, then turn the bird over and press down to flatten it. Or ask your butcher to do this for you.

SERVES 4 | PREP 20 MINS | SOAK 1 HR | COOKING 6½ HRS | SETTING LOW & HIGH

An Italian-influenced dish that makes good use of a good-value bird. It works just as well with chicken breast, but you lose the wow factor.

Italian poussin with white beans

2 tbsp raisins

7 tbsp sweet wine, eg *vin santo*

2 large free-range poussin, split in half

2 tbsp red wine vinegar

4 tbsp olive oil

4 Italian sausages or your favorite meaty sausages, ideally flavored with fennel

1 onion, finely chopped

1 tsp soft thyme leaves

1 celery stalk, finely diced

1 garlic clove, crushed to a paste with a little sea salt

1 bay leaf

8oz can chopped tomatoes

2 tbsp superfine sugar

14oz can cannellini, navy, or great Northern beans, drained and rinsed

2 tbsp pine nuts, toasted

1. Place the raisins in a bowl with 3 tbsp sweet wine, cover, and leave to soak for at least 1 hour but preferably overnight.

2. Snip out the ribcage in the poussin halves, leaving the breast attached to the leg and thigh.

3. Place the poussin in a bowl and pour over the wine vinegar, 3 tbsp olive oil, and the remaining sweet wine. Cover and set aside to marinate for 15 minutes, then drain, reserving the marinade.

4. Warm the remaining tbsp olive oil in a large skillet over high heat, then brown the sausages and poussin. Remove and set aside. Add the onion, thyme, celery, garlic, and bay leaf and fry over low heat for 6–8 minutes, stirring from time to time. Spoon into the slow cooker. Add the marinade, tomatoes, and sugar with about ¼ cup water, then cover and cook on low for 6 hours until the meat is cooked through.

5. Lift out the poussin and sausages onto a warm platter. Cover and keep warm. Add the beans, raisins with their soaking liquid, and pine nuts to the cooking juices in the slow cooker. Turn to high, cover with a lid, and cook for 20 minutes. Return the poussin and sausages to the sauce, cover, and heat through for a further 10 minutes.

SERVING SUGGESTION
This is a one-pot supper, but a salad or green vegetable is good with it, too.

SERVES
4

PREP
20 MINS

COOKING
4½–6½
HRS

SETTING
LOW &
HIGH

Why oh why don't we eat more game birds? They are nutritious, very low in saturated fat, and the taste is fabulous. This recipe could also be used for pheasant, in which case double the cooking time on low and use two birds instead of four.

Pot-roasted partridge with hard cider and Calvados

4 tbsp butter

4 partridge

salt and freshly ground black pepper

1 medium onion, diced

3oz bacon, diced

1 celery stalk, coarsely chopped

1 carrot, coarsely chopped

4 sage sprigs

1 Granny Smith apple, peeled, cored, and cut into large chunks

1 Bramley apple, peeled, cored, and cut into large chunks

¼ cup Calvados, plus 2 tbsp

1¼ cups hard dry cider

⅔ cup heavy cream

4 tbsp finely chopped flat-leaf parsley

1 tsp finely chopped tarragon

to serve

buttered cabbage

new potatoes

1. Melt the butter in a large skillet. Season the partridge and fry over medium heat until pale golden all over. Remove with long-handled tongs and place in your slow cooker.

2. Add the onion, lardons, celery, carrot, and sage sprigs to the skillet and cook over medium heat for about 8 minutes, until the onion is soft and translucent and the lardons are crisp. Carefully pour off any excess fat that has emerged from the lardons, then add the vegetable mixture to the slow cooker.

3. Sprinkle over the apple chunks, then pour over ¼ cup Calvados. Set the Calvados alight then, once the flames have died down, add the hard cider. Cover the slow cooker with the lid and cook on low for 4–6 hours until the meat is cooked.

4. Push the sauce through a fine-meshed sieve into a bowl. Pour this strained sauce back into the slow cooker, add 2 tbsp Calvados, increase the heat to high, and cook, uncovered, for 20 minutes. Add the cream and whisk together. Cover and cook for a further 10 minutes until the sauce is creamy and slightly thickened. Fold in the parsley and tarragon and season to taste.

5. Spoon the sauce over the partridge and serve with buttered cabbage and new potatoes.

SERVING SUGGESTION
Peel and core 1lb all-purpose apples and cut each apple into 8 segments. Pan-fry in 2 tbsp unsalted butter with ⅓ cup soft dark brown sugar over medium heat for about 8 minutes, turning from time to time, until golden. Serve immediately with the partridge.

SERVES
4

PREP
15 MINS

MARINATE
1 HR

COOKING
2½–3
HRS

SETTING
LOW

The humble wild pigeon requires a little love and effort to extract its best qualities but, of course, you could always buy expensive corn-fed squab if you want more of a dinner-party dish.

Braised pigeon with pine nuts and raisins

4 pigeons, cleaned

4 tbsp red wine vinegar

6 tbsp olive oil

⅔ cup *vin santo* or other sweet wine

4oz smoked bacon, diced
or pancetta pieces

1 onion, finely chopped

1 carrot, diced

2 celery stalks, diced

2 garlic cloves, crushed

1 bay leaf

4 tbsp raisins

2 tbsp pine nuts, toasted

to serve

green vegetables

mashed potatoes

1. Split the pigeons in half, cutting through and removing the breastbone, so that you have 8 pieces. Place the pigeons in a nonmetallic bowl. Pour over the wine vinegar, 3 tbsp olive oil, and 2 tbsp of the *vin santo*. Cover and set aside to marinate for at least 1 hour at room temperature, or overnight in the fridge. Drain.

2. Warm the remaining 3 tbsp olive oil in a skillet. Add the bacon, onion, carrot, celery, garlic, and bay leaf and fry over low heat for 8–10 minutes until the vegetables are starting to color. Stir to combine.

3. Lay the pigeon halves in the slow cooker, add the vegetable mixture, and the remaining *vin santo* plus the marinade and ⅓ cup water, then cover and cook on low for 2½–3 hours until the meat is cooked through.

4. Meanwhile, soak the raisins in warm water for 20 minutes, then drain.

5. Lift the pigeon halves onto a warm platter. Add the raisins and pine nuts to the pan juices and vegetables, then spoon over the pigeon.

6. Serve with green vegetables and mashed potatoes.

SERVES
4

PREP
25 MINS

MARINATE
8 HRS

COOKING
6¾–7¾
HRS

SETTING
LOW &
HIGH

Here in the UK, hare is fast disappearing from the culinary repertoire, which is a shame. However, it is still plentiful in parts of the US, so here is a delicious one-pot dish inspired by the Spanish Tolosa bean (Basque black bean) stews.

Braised hare with Tolosa beans

8 hare pieces, preferably haunch legs
salt and freshly ground black pepper

for the marinade
1 tsp finely chopped soft thyme leaves
1 bay leaf
1 onion, finely sliced
1 garlic clove, finely chopped
2 tbsp Armagnac

for the beans
1 onion, finely chopped
2 garlic cloves, finely chopped
½ cup extra-virgin olive oil
pinch of cayenne pepper
½lb chorizo sausage, sliced into
   1in chunks
½lb blood sausage, cut into
   1in chunks
14oz can red kidney beans,
   rinsed and drained
¼lb smoked bacon, diced
2½ cups chicken stock or water
1½lb Savoy cabbage, shredded

to serve
creamy mashed potatoes
gremolata (see page 84)

1. Wash the hare pieces, place them in a bowl, and mix with all the marinade ingredients, then season to taste. Cover with plastic wrap, refrigerate, and marinate for at least 8 hours, turning from time to time.

2. For the beans, gently fry the onion and the garlic in half the oil with the cayenne for about 8 minutes, until the onion has softened but not browned.

3. Increase the heat, add the chorizo and blood sausage, and cook for 5 minutes to release the fat.

4. Add the hare pieces to the pan and brown all over. Spoon into your slow cooker, then stir in the beans, bacon, sausage mixture, and stock. Cover and cook on low for 6–7 hours.

5. Turn the slow cooker to high, then add the cabbage and cook for a further 40 minutes.

6. Spoon the beans and meat into 4 warm bowls and serve with creamy mashed potatoes and a sprinkling of gremolata.

SERVES
4

PREP
20 MINS

SOAK
12 HRS

COOKING
5¼–6¼ HRS

SETTING
LOW & HIGH

A classic French combination, the sorrel adds citrusy notes, which help to cut the richness of the sweetbreads. If you can order the sweetbreads through a decent butcher you'll find this dish easy and delicious.

Braised sweetbreads with sorrel

4 calves' sweetbreads, soaked for 12 hours in several changes of cold water

3 carrots, thinly sliced

2 celery stalks, thinly sliced

16 baby onions, peeled

4 tbsp unsalted butter

2 garlic cloves, finely chopped

1 tsp soft thyme leaves

14oz can chopped tomatoes

½ cup dry white wine

½ cup chicken stock

1¼ cups frozen petits pois, defrosted

½lb jumbo shrimp, peeled

3 handfuls sorrel

⅔ cup heavy cream

salt and freshly ground black pepper

to serve

mashed potatoes

1. Blanch the sweetbreads in boiling salted water for 5 minutes, plunge into cold water, then remove all the sinews and transparent skin and leave whole.

2. In a skillet, gently cook the carrots, celery, and onions in half the butter for 10 minutes. Add the garlic, thyme, and sweetbreads and fry until the sweetbreads are lightly colored. Transfer the mixture to your slow cooker and add the tomatoes, white wine, and stock, then cover and cook on a low setting for 5–6 hours until the sweetbreads are cooked.

3. Turn the slow cooker to high, add the peas and shrimp, cover, and cook for 15 minutes. Remove the sweetbreads, shrimp, and vegetables and keep warm.

4. Meanwhile, place the remaining butter in a pan over low heat. Add the sorrel and cook, stirring occasionally, until it has broken down.

5. Strain the cooking juices from the slow cooker onto the sorrel and boil until the sauce has reduced by half. Stir in the cream and season to taste. Return the solids to the sauce and cook, uncovered, for a further 15 minutes.

6. Slice the sweetbreads and arrange on 4 warm plates with the shrimp and vegetables. Spoon the sauce over the shrimp and vegetables and serve with mashed potatoes.

Also try

If you can't find sorrel, try using spinach with lemon juice. Note that the spinach won't break down like the sorrel in step 4 so will need liquidizing.

SERVES
4

PREP
20 MINS

COOKING
8–10 HRS

SETTING
LOW

The arrival of new-season lamb heralds the start of the growing season—longer evenings, the sun brings warmth, time to tend the garden—and so here I bring the two together using a good-value cut and some lovely baby vegetables.

Spring lamb with vegetables

2 tbsp olive oil

8 lamb shoulder steaks (about 1½lb)

4 cloves

12 baby shallots, peeled

2 small leeks, thickly sliced, white and green parts kept separate

1 fennel bulb, tough outer layer removed, halved, and sliced

2 tbsp all-purpose flour

¾ cup red wine

2½ cups lamb stock

8 juniper berries

salt and freshly ground black pepper

1lb baby new potatoes

1 head of garlic, cut in half horizontally

1 bouquet garni

½lb baby Chantenay carrots, trimmed and scrubbed

8 baby turnips, tops trimmed to about ½in

½ small Savoy cabbage, cut into quarters

to serve
salsa verde (optional)

1. Heat the oil in a large skillet, add the lamb, and brown on both sides over high heat for about 6 minutes. Lift out and put on a plate.

2. Press the cloves into 4 shallots, then add all the shallots, the white sliced leeks (reserve the green slices for later), and fennel to the skillet. Cook for 3–4 minutes over medium heat until just beginning to brown, then sprinkle over the flour and mix together. Cook for a further 2–3 minutes, stirring regularly. Stir in the red wine, stock, juniper berries, and plenty of seasoning, and bring to a boil.

3. Put the potatoes in the base of the slow cooker, arrange the lamb steaks on top, then tuck in the halved garlic head and bouquet garni. Pour over the vegetable and hot wine mixture. Cover and cook on low for 8–10 hours, until the lamb is cooked and the potatoes are tender.

4. When you are almost ready to serve, boil the carrots and turnips for 8–10 minutes; steam the cabbage for 8–10 minutes and the green leek tops (but don't mix with the cabbage) for the last 3 minutes, until all the vegetables are just tender.

5. Drain the vegetables and stir the carrots, turnips, and leeks into the lamb. Ladle into shallow soup bowls and serve the cabbage to one side. For extra punch, serve the lamb topped with spoonfuls of salsa verde (see below).

FOR THE SALSA VERDE

In a food processor, blitz 3 garlic cloves, 3 sliced scallions, 2 finely chopped fresh green chiles, 3 chopped anchovy fillets in oil (drained), 3 tbsp capers (rinsed), and a small bunch each of cilantro and parsley, until finely chopped. Add 1½ tbsp lemon juice, 1½ tbsp red wine and a scant cup fresh white breadcrumbs. Slowly mix in up to ¾ cup olive oil to make a coarse sauce similar to pesto in texture. Season to taste and chill.

Antony's tips
Lamb neck pieces can be used instead of shoulder steaks because many people don't like the bones. Neck tastes delicious and is a great budget cut.

SERVES
4

PREP
20 MINS

COOKING
6 HRS

SETTING
LOW

A classic partnership of lamb with rosemary and a complete dish with no other additions necessary. If flageolet beans are not available, feel free to use white cannellini, navy, or great Northern beans.

Lamb steaks with rosemary garlic flageolet crust

2 tbsp good olive oil

4 slices smoked bacon, diced

4 garlic cloves, finely chopped

3 anchovies in oil, drained and roughly chopped

2 onions, roughly chopped

1 carrot, roughly chopped

1 celery stalk, finely chopped

1 tbsp rosemary leaves, very finely chopped

2 x 14oz cans flageolet beans, drained and rinsed

salt and freshly ground black pepper

4 tbsp unsalted butter

4 lamb leg steaks

⅔ cup red wine

⅔ cup lamb stock

4 tbsp fresh white breadcrumbs

½ cup Parmesan, grated

1. In a skillet, heat half the olive oil, add the bacon, and cook for 5 minutes over medium heat. Add the garlic, anchovies, onions, carrot, celery, and rosemary and gently cook for 8 minutes, stirring occasionally, until the onion has softened. Add the beans and combine. Season and set aside.

2. In the same skillet, heat the remaining olive oil and butter and cook the lamb steaks over high heat for 3 minutes on each side, until they are lightly browned.

3. Spoon a layer of the bean mixture into your slow cooker, place the lamb steaks on top, then add the remaining beans. Pour in the wine and stock, cover, and cook on low for 6 hours until the meat is cooked.

4. Mix together the breadcrumbs and Parmesan and scatter over the beans. Place the slow cooker pot under a hot broiler to brown.

SERVES
6–8

PREP
20 MINS

MARINATE
2 HRS

COOKING
2½ HRS

OVEN

This is roast lamb with attitude. Loads of garlic, hints of chile, and the aroma of lemon all go toward making this roast lamb dish just that little bit different.

Arabian roast lamb and potatoes

1 leg of lamb

6 garlic cloves, halved

2 tbsp rose harissa paste

juice and grated zest of 1 unwaxed or
    organic lemon

pinch of saffron strands, soaked in
    1 tbsp very hot water

1 tsp mint leaves

1 tbsp cilantro leaves

4 tbsp olive oil

1lb potatoes, cut into ½in slices

2 large onions, thickly sliced

salt and freshly ground black pepper

to serve

couscous

spinach

plain yogurt

1. Make a dozen incisions in the lamb about ¾in deep and long.

2. In a mini food processor or mortar and pestle, blend the garlic, harissa, lemon juice and zest, saffron and water, mint, cilantro, and half the oil to a rough paste. Spread three-quarters of this paste over the lamb, pushing it into the cuts. Place the lamb in a large bowl and cover with plastic wrap. Refrigerate and leave to marinate for at least 2 hours, but ideally overnight.

3. Preheat the oven to 350°F.

4. Mix the potatoes, onions, and the remaining oil and spice paste together and transfer to a roasting pan, then place the lamb on top. Season well and roast in the oven for 2 hours until the meat is cooked, basting from time to time and turning the potatoes and onions.

5. Remove from the oven and lift out the lamb onto a platter. Cover with foil and rest in a warm place for 15–20 minutes.

6. Increase the oven temperature to 400°F and return the roasting pan to the oven for about 20 minutes more to brown the potatoes.

7. Drizzle with yogurt, and serve with couscous and spinach.

SERVES
4

PREP
30 MINS

COOKING
9½ HRS

SETTING
LOW &
HIGH

I use mutton here because I love it and, with its really bold flavor, it's perfect for slow cooking. You may have trouble sourcing mutton, so unless you know a good butcher, feel free to use a shoulder of lamb instead.

North African mutton with spiced fruits and nuts

½ cup prunes, stoned and halved

⅔ cup dried apricots, quartered

1¼ cups strong black tea, hot

2 tbsp argan oil or vegetable oil

2¼lb shoulder of mutton, most of the fat removed, cut into 2in chunks

2 onions, finely chopped

½ tsp ground turmeric

½ tsp ground ginger

¼ tsp grated nutmeg

1½ tsp ground cinnamon

pinch of saffron strands

2 tsp harissa paste

2 tbsp runny honey

¾ cups hot lamb or beef stock

4 tbsp plain, strained yogurt

1 tbsp finely chopped mint

½ cup flaked almonds, toasted

3 tbsp roughly chopped cilantro

1. Soak the prunes and apricots in the tea for 30 minutes, stirring from time to time.

2. Put half the oil in a skillet over high heat, add the mutton, and brown all over. Remove and set aside.

3. Add the remaining oil to the skillet and fry the onions over medium heat for about 8 minutes, until soft and lightly golden. Add the spices, stir to combine, and cook for 1 minute. Spoon this mixture into your slow cooker and top with the mutton and soaked fruits and their liquid.

4. Stir in two-thirds of the harissa, two-thirds of the honey, and all the stock, cover, and cook on high for 1½ hours, then turn the slow cooker to low, cover again, and cook for a further 8 hours, until the meat is cooked.

5. Meanwhile, combine the remaining harissa and honey with the yogurt and mint and refrigerate until needed.

6. Sprinkle the stew with the almonds and cilantro, and serve with the yogurt on the side.

Aragan oil
Argan oil has a unique, nutty taste. Most of it comes from southern Morocco, where Berber women constantly race the local goats, which have a remarkable tree-climbing ability, to collect the prized nuts of the argan tree.

SERVES
4–6

PREP
20 MINS

COOKING
6½–8½
HRS

SETTING
LOW &
HIGH

This is quite a gourmet dish, but then I am a chef, so you would expect me to run to a couple of quirky dishes. If you love liver, you'll go for this one. If you prefer lamb's liver, reduce the cooking time on low to 4–6 hours.

Braised calf's liver

1 tbsp olive oil

2 tbsp butter

2¼lb piece of calf's liver, cut
   from the thickest section

salt and freshly ground black pepper

6oz smoked bacon, cut into lardons

1 large onion, roughly chopped

3 large carrots, roughly sliced

1 leek, thinly sliced

4 garlic cloves, roughly chopped

8oz can chopped tomatoes

2 bay leaves

2 thyme sprigs

1 celery stalk, thinly sliced

½ bottle red wine

1 tsp superfine sugar

1 tbsp Worcestershire sauce

2 tbsp brandy (optional)

2 tbsp finely chopped flat-leaf parsley

to serve

buttered peas

mashed potatoes

1. Put the oil and butter in a skillet over high heat and brown the liver all over. Season and set aside.

2. Add the bacon to the skillet and cook over medium heat for 8–10 minutes, until golden, then remove half and set aside.

3. Add the onion, carrots, leek, and garlic to the bacon in the skillet and cook for a further 6–8 minutes to soften and color the vegetables. Spoon into your slow cooker. Add the liver, tomatoes, herbs, celery, wine, sugar, and Worcestershire sauce. Stir to combine, then cover, and cook on low for 6–8 hours, until the liver is cooked.

4. Remove the liver, cover with foil, and keep warm. There should be plenty of juices in the slow cooker pot. Liquidize the juices with the vegetables and bacon, then pass though a fine sieve and return to the slow cooker with the liver and reserved bacon. Cover and cook on high for 20 minutes. Add the brandy, if using, and parsley and stir to combine.

5. Carve the liver into slices, whatever thickness you like, spoon over the sauce and serve with buttered peas and mashed potatoes.

SERVES
4

PREP
30 MINS

COOKING
8¼ HRS

SETTING
LOW &
HIGH

Even before I discovered the merits of the slow cooker, I loved
pot-roasts, as they're perfect for one-pot dining. If gremolata is not
for you, serve this with a dollop of pesto mixed with sour cream.

Pot-roasted beef with gremolata

¼ cup olive oil

4 small potatoes, unpeeled,
washed, and halved

2 parsnips, peeled and roughly chopped
in ¾in pieces

¾lb butternut squash, unpeeled, seeded,
and cut into 4 wedges

¾lb baby Chantenay carrots,
trimmed and scrubbed

12 baby onions, peeled whole, leaving
as much of the root on as possible

2lb piece of beef rump, boneless chuck
or brisket

2 tbsp wholegrain mustard

6 garlic cloves, peeled

12 thyme sprigs

1 tbsp smoked paprika

sea salt and freshly ground black pepper

1 tbsp Worcestershire sauce

1 tbsp tomato paste

1½ cups beef stock

½ cup red wine

1 tbsp gravy thickener

for the gremolata

2 tbsp finely chopped flat-leaf parsley

1 garlic clove, finely chopped

grated zest of 1 unwaxed or organic
lemon

1. Heat the oil in a skillet over medium heat and cook in batches the
potatoes, parsnips, butternut squash, carrots, and onions, until golden
brown. Spoon this mixture into the bottom of your slow cooker.

2. In the same pan with the residual oil, fry the beef until brown all over.

3. Meanwhile, in a mini food processor, blend together the mustard, garlic,
thyme, and paprika with a little sea salt until smooth, then stir in the
Worcestershire sauce and tomato paste.

4. Spread this mixture over the beef, then place the meat on top of the
vegetables. Add the beef stock and wine, cover, and cook on low for 8 hours
until the beef is cooked through.

5. Remove the beef, cover loosely with foil, and set aside to rest.

6. Turn the cooker to high. Whisk the gravy thickener with 2 tbsp water
and stir it into the liquid and vegetables in the cooker. Cover and cook for
15 minutes until lightly thickened. Check the seasoning.

7. Slice the beef and arrange on 4 warm plates, then top with the
vegetables and sauce. Combine the ingredients for the gremolata and
sprinkle over each portion.

Gravy tip
After thickening the sauce, add 1 tbsp verjuice or balsamic vinegar for
a taste explosion.

SERVES
4

PREP
20 MINS

COOKING
8½–10½
HRS

SETTING
LOW &
HIGH

Using the cheaper cuts of meat is a dying skill, but if we don't buy the animal's forequarters it means the price of its hindquarters—the luxury end—keeps going up. And there is always the bonus of a magical flavor. Chuck steak, which is used here, is a perfect cut for braising in your slow cooker.

Braised beef with baby carrots and horseradish

4 x 8oz chuck steaks

¼ cup seasoned all-purpose flour

2 tbsp beef dripping, lard, or
vegetable oil

2 onions, roughly chopped

1 celery stalk, finely sliced

1 thyme sprig

2 bay leaves

2 tbsp unsalted butter

2 garlic cloves, crushed to a paste with
a little sea salt

½ tsp crushed juniper berries

2 tsp mild curry powder or paste

1 tbsp dark muscovado sugar

2 cups good beef stock, boiling or hot

1 tbsp Worcestershire sauce

3 tbsp grated horseradish in vinegar,
drained

16 baby Chantenay carrots, trimmed
and scrubbed

1 heaping cup frozen petits pois,
defrosted

salt and freshly ground black pepper

to serve
mashed or new potatoes

1. Coat the chuck steaks in the seasoned flour on both sides, shaking off any excess.

2. Heat half the dripping in a skillet to almost smoking, then fry the steaks quickly on both sides until nicely browned. Remove and set aside.

3. Add the remaining dripping to the skillet, now over medium heat, and fry the onions, celery, thyme, and bay leaf leaves for 8–10 minutes, until the onion has softened and turned a pale golden color.

4. Add the butter with the garlic, juniper berries, curry powder, and sugar, stir to combine, and cook for 2–3 minutes until aromatic. Transfer the mixture to your slow cooker, top with the steaks, and stir in the remaining ingredients, except the peas. Cover and cook on low for 8–10 hours.

5. Turn the slow cooker to high, add the peas, season, then cover and cook for a further 20 minutes. Serve with mashed or new potatoes.

Antony's tips
For the seasoned flour I like to add salt, pepper, a pinch of celery salt, and ½ tsp English mustard powder.

SERVES
4

PREP
30 MINS

COOKING
3¾–4¾
HRS

SETTING
LOW &
HIGH

I know you're thinking, "But I don't like prunes." Nor did I, but it's funny, when you partner pork with prunes they make the perfect marriage, and the great thing about pork is that it is such good value.

Pork fillets with prune and parsley stuffing

2 tbsp unsalted butter

2 shallots, very finely chopped

4 dried apricots, finely chopped

1 celery stalk, very finely chopped

4 tbsp finely chopped parsley

2 tsp finely chopped mint

2 tbsp extra-virgin olive oil

1 scant cup fresh white breadcrumbs

3 tbsp pine nuts, toasted and finely chopped

grated zest of 1 organic orange

salt and freshly ground black pepper

8 prunes, pitted

2 x 8oz pork tenderloins, silverskin (shiny membrane) removed

6 slices of Parma ham

¾ dry white wine

sage leaves

to serve

cabbage or green beans

mashed potatoes

1. Heat the butter in a skillet, then gently cook the shallots, apricots, and celery for about 10 minutes, until soft. Transfer to a bowl and add the parsley, mint, half the oil, the breadcrumbs, pine nuts, and orange zest. Mix together and season. Shape this stuffing into 8 small balls, which you squeeze into the center of each split prune.

2. Split the pork tenderloins lengthways by cutting three-quarters of the way through. Open each up like a book, then cover the cut side with plastic wrap and bash evenly with a meat mallet or a rolling pin until the meat is about ¼in thick.

3. Arrange 3 slices of slightly overlapping Parma ham on a board and place a flattened pork tenderloin on top, cut-side up. Arrange 4 stuffed prunes down the length of the pork, and then roll up completely, enclosing the pork in Parma ham. Secure with 3 toothpicks. Repeat with the other piece.

4. Heat the remaining oil in a skillet and brown the fillets all over on high heat. Remove and place in the bottom of your slow cooker.

5. Pour the wine into the skillet, scrape, and stir up any sticky bits, and bring to a boil. Pour over the pork, then cover and cook on low for 3–4 hours.

6. Add the sage to the slow cooker, increase the temperature to high, cover, and cook for 40 minutes, until the meat is cooked.

7. Remove the pork and carve each fillet into 4. Arrange 2 slices on each plate, spoon over the cooking juices, and serve with cabbage or green beans and mashed potatoes.

Also try
If you wish, use chicken breasts instead of the pork, and cook for the same length of time.

SERVES
4

PREP
20 MINS

COOKING
8½–10½
HRS

SETTING
LOW &
HIGH

In my earlier life I was never a fan of fruit in savory cooking, but then I discovered Morocco and fell in love with tagines. This recipe has little to do with Morocco, but it has similar influences.

Garlic and sage pork with fennel and pears

2¾lb boneless rolled pork shoulder

1 tbsp olive oil

2 tbsp fennel seeds

1 tsp dried oregano

1 tsp dried rosemary

3 tbsp wholegrain Dijon mustard

1 tsp sea salt

1 tsp crushed black peppercorns

1 head of garlic, broken into cloves
   and lightly smashed with the back
   of a knife

1 bunch sage, tied with string

2/3 cup chicken stock

2/3 cup dry perry (pear cider)

2 tsp runny honey

2 Bartlett pears, peeled, cored, and
   cut into wedges

to serve

creamy mashed potatoes

green vegetables

1. Tie the pork with kitchen twine to create a more uniform shape. Heat the oil in a skillet and brown the pork all over on high heat, remove, and allow to cool.

2. In a mortar and pestle or electric coffee grinder, crush the fennel, oregano, and rosemary to a powder, then set aside.

3. Paint the pork all over with the mustard, then sprinkle with the fennel mixture and the salt and pepper. Place the pork carefully in the slow cooker and add the garlic, sage, stock, perry, and honey, then place the pears around the meat.

4. Cover and cook on low for 8–10 hours, until the meat is cooked. Remove the pork from the cooker, cover with foil, and rest in a warm place while you turn the cooker to high to reduce the juices slightly. Cook, uncovered, for 25 minutes.

5. Carve the pork, then return it to the cooker for 10 minutes to warm through. Serve with the pears, the juices, some creamy mashed potatoes, and a green vegetable, perhaps green beans.

Also try
Feel free to replace the pears and perry and use instead tart all-purpose apples, and a glug of apple cider.

SERVES
4

PREP
30 MINS

MARINATE
OVER-
NIGHT

COOKING
6–7 HRS

SETTING
HIGH

All my family love this dish and its delicious balance between sweet and pepper. Look no further for perfect comfort food on a chilly day, when your body needs a little TLC.

Spicy pork in stout

3¼lb piece of boneless thick
   end pork belly, skin removed

6 Kalamata olives, stoned

6 sage leaves

6 stoned prunes

6 anchovy fillets in oil, drained

2 tbsp olive oil

2 tbsp butter

2 onions, cut into thick wedges

2 tbsp all-purpose flour

11fl oz Guinness or stout

1¼ cups chicken stock

for the marinade

2 tsp crushed black peppercorns

1 tsp salt

2 tsp dried oregano

1 tsp soft thyme leaves

7 garlic cloves, peeled

3 tbsp soft brown sugar

2 tbsp olive oil

2 tbsp red wine vinegar

to serve

mashed potatoes

baby fava beans

finely chopped fresh herbs
   (e.g. parsley, chives)

1. Turn the pork so that the underside is uppermost on a cutting board. Make 12 deep incisions distributed evenly over the meat's surface. Wrap each olive in a sage leaf and stuff each prune with a rolled-up anchovy fillet. Press these into the pork incisions.

2. Put all the marinade ingredients into a mini food processor and blend to a smooth paste. Pour half into the base of a shallow nonmetallic dish, add the pork so that it lies flat, then rub the rest of the marinade over the top. Cover with plastic wrap and refrigerate overnight.

3. Scrape some of the excess marinade from the pork and reserve, then roll up the pork from one of the short ends with the "stuffed" side innermost, and tie at intervals along its length with twine.

4. Heat the oil in a skillet over high heat, add the pork, and fry, turning, until evenly browned, adding the butter and onions halfway through. Lift the pork into your slow cooker.

5. Stir the flour into the pan, cook gently for 3 minutes, stirring regularly, then mix in the remaining marinade, Guinness, and stock. Bring to a boil, scraping and stirring up the bits from the base of the pan, then transfer the mixture to the slow cooker. Cover and cook on high for 6–7 hours until the pork is cooked and very tender.

6. Transfer the pork to a serving plate, cut into thick slices, and discard the twine. Serve with spoonfuls of the Guinness sauce, mashed potatoes, and baby fava beans tossed with chopped fresh herbs.

Slow cooker tips
It is important that large pieces of pork are cooked only on the high setting and submerged in liquid so they cook evenly. If you would prefer the finished sauce to be thicker, purée the onions and sauce, then transfer to a wide shallow pan and boil rapidly for 5 minutes or so until it has reduced to your liking.

SERVES
4

PREP
15 MINS

COOKING
7–8 HRS

SETTING
HIGH

This is a really useful meat recipe because, although it satisfying just as it is with mashed potatoes or a bowl of lentils, it's also a great standby for soups, salads, and stews. Think of this recipe as a foundation for bigger things. You can add potatoes, root vegetables, chorizo, clams, tomatoes—the choice is yours.

Poached pork shoulder

1 large onion, thinly sliced
1 carrot, thinly sliced
3¼lb boneless pork shoulder
½ bottle dry white wine
2 cups chicken stock
1 tsp sea salt
2 tsp finely chopped fresh ginger
1 tsp black peppercorns
4 dried chiles
1 clove
1 tbsp clear honey
1 star anise
1 bulb of garlic, cut in half horizontally
2 tsp coriander seeds
1 tsp cumin seeds
2 bay leaves
2 celery stalks, thinly sliced
2 tbsp roughly chopped cilantro leaves

to serve
hot Puy lentils or mashed potatoes
Dijon mustard

1. Place the sliced onion and carrot in your slow cooker with the pork on top. Add all the remaining ingredients.

2. Cover and cook on high for 7–8 hours until the meat is cooked. Halfway through cooking, turn the pork over. Remove the meat from the stock.

3. Serve the hot pork with lentils or mashed potatoes and some good strong mustard.

Using the stock
If serving the pork cold, allow the meat to cool in the stock. When cold, take out the meat, strain the stock through muslin, and remove the fat. This is a good base for sauces or soups and can be frozen for up to 6 months.

SERVES
4–6

PREP
10 MINS

SOAK
4 HRS

COOKING
6½–8½ HRS

SETTING
HIGH

With an Irish wife, many a meal has included gammon (a delicious cut of cured ham that is perfect for a quick roast) and potatoes, so finding variations can be a challenge. This one was inspired by a recipe from one of Britain's top chefs, Phil Vickery.

Braised gammon and potatoes with a peach and Barkham Blue cheese sauce

2¼lb gammon (country-cured ham),
  soaked in cold water for 4 hours
2¼lb potatoes, cut into ¼in slices
2 onions, finely sliced
1 tbsp soft thyme leaves
salt and freshly ground black pepper
2 tbsp butter
12 baby carrots, trimmed and scrubbed
2 bay leaves
¾ cup chicken stock
¾ cup peach juice

for the sauce
14oz can peach halves in juice, drained
⅔ cup heavy cream
4½oz Barkham Blue (or another
  blue cheese), crumbled

to serve
green beans

1. Place the gammon in a large saucepan, cover with cold water, and bring to a boil. Reduce the heat, cover with a lid, and simmer for 30 minutes. Layer the potatoes and onions in the bottom of your slow cooker, sprinkle with the thyme, then season and dot the top with the butter.

2. Remove the gammon from the saucepan and nestle in the potato layers. Add the baby carrots and bay leaves. Pour in the stock and peach juice, then cover and cook on high for 6–8 hours, until the meat is cooked.

3. Meanwhile, to make the sauce, whiz the peaches in a food processor until smooth. In a small pan, gently heat the cream and cheese until melted. Stir in the peach purée and heat through. (This can be made in advance.)

4. Remove the gammon and carve. Spoon the potatoes and onions onto warm plates and arrange the meat on top. Serve with the sauce on the side and green beans.

SERVES
4

PREP
15 MINS

COOKING
7 HRS

SETTING
LOW &
HIGH

Even big children love spareribs and these are beautifully sticky and flavorsome. The slow cooking produces a very tender result, perfect for just finishing off on the barbecue.

Caramelized spareribs with bourbon and ginger

2 racks of baby back pork ribs

1 cup bourbon

¼ cup thinly sliced fresh ginger

4 garlic cloves

2 long fresh red chiles

4 cups chicken stock

2 tbsp vegetable oil

for the sauce

2 garlic cloves, crushed to a paste with a little sea salt

2 tsp grated fresh ginger

½ tsp dried red pepper flakes

¾ cup soft dark brown sugar

½ cup rice vinegar

1 cup good tomato ketchup

to serve

baked potatoes

home-made apple coleslaw

1. Place the ribs in a slow cooker with the bourbon, sliced ginger, garlic, chiles, and stock. Cover and cook on low for 6 hours until the meat is cooked through.

2. Remove the ribs and set aside, increase the heat to high, leave uncovered, and cook the liquor for 45 minutes or until reduced by half.

3. Meanwhile, brush the cooked ribs with the oil and fry in a large skillet over high heat until brown all over. Set aside.

4. Preheat your broiler to high or oven to 425°F, or have your barbecue ready. Combine the reduced cooking juices with the sauce ingredients and paint this sauce over the ribs. Cook the ribs until nicely glazed (be careful, they burn easily), turning the ribs a couple of times and continuing to paint to build up a glaze.

5. Serve with baked potatoes and hand-made apple coleslaw.

FOR THE APPLE COLESLAW
For the apple coleslaw: whisk together 1 garlic clove crushed to a paste with sea salt, 2 anchovy fillets in oil (drained and mashed to a paste), ½ cup good-quality mayonnaise, ½ cup plain, strained yogurt, 2 tsp Dijon mustard and 1 tbsp finely chopped dill. Set aside. Whisk 2 tbsp white wine vinegar with 2 tsp golden superfine sugar and toss with ½ large Savoy cabbage, shredded. Leave for 1 hour. Fold in 2 cored and diced apples, then add enough dressing to coat and mix well. Season to taste, cover, and chill for 1 hour before serving.

Also try
Replace the bourbon with 1 cup dark soy sauce for a more Asian set of spareribs.

Bakes

Steak and kidney pudding

see page 112

A perfect supper dish that ticks all the boxes. It's excellent with poached eggs or as an accompaniment to grilled or roast meat or fish.

Vegetable and red pepper gratin

4 sliced smoked bacon, diced

2 tbsp unsalted butter

2 leeks, shredded

½ red pepper, cored, seeded, and chopped

14oz can corn, drained

salt and freshly ground black pepper

4 egg yolks

1 tsp English mustard powder

2½ cups heavy cream

½ tsp Tabasco

½ tsp Worcestershire sauce

1. Cook the bacon with the butter in a skillet over medium heat for about 3 minutes until crisp. Add the leeks and red pepper and cook for a further 5 minutes, stirring occasionally. Add the corn and stir to combine. Season and put the mixture into your slow cooker.

2. In a bowl, beat together the egg yolks, mustard, cream, Tabasco and Worcestershire sauce. Season again with salt and pepper and pour over the corn mixture.

3. Cover and cook on low for 2–3 hours, until a knife inserted into the center of the gratin comes out clean.

How to check if the gratin is cooked
To check if the gratin is cooked without lifting the lid too often, look through the lid to see if it appears to be cooked. Then, if it does, carefully shake the slow cooker. There should be a firm wobble rather than loose liquid.

SERVES
4

PREP
15 MINS

COOKING
4 HRS

SETTING
HIGH

This is a blast from the past, very popular in the 1980s—the era of nouvelle cuisine—when you might receive six or seven stuffed vegetables as a vegetarian main course. Back then, they would have been miniature vegetables, whereas these stuffed onions are far more robust.

Onions stuffed with tomatos, garlic, and mozzarella

2 large Spanish onions, whole and unpeeled

1 heaping cup fresh white breadcrumbs

2 tbsp olive oil, plus extra for greasing

3 garlic cloves, roughly chopped

4 tbsp finely chopped curly-leaf parsley

2 tbsp freshly grated Parmesan

1 tsp soft thyme leaves

salt and freshly ground black pepper

8 sun-dried tomatoes, roughly chopped

8oz-ball mozzarella, cut into ¼in dice

2 tbsp pine nuts

⅔ cup vegetable stock, boiling or hot

1. Cook the whole onions in boiling salted water for 15 minutes, drain, and when cool enough to handle, cut in half horizontally and peel.

2. Use a melon baller or teaspoon to remove about 4 layers of onion from the center of each half and reserve, leaving a thick layer of onion with an intact base. Slice a very small amount off the base of each onion half, so it can stand flat.

3. Meanwhile, in a mini food processor, blend together the breadcrumbs, oil, garlic, parsley, Parmesan, and thyme.

4. Finely chop half of the reserved onion centers, season to taste, and fold them into the breadcrumb mix with the tomatoes, mozzarella, and pine nuts. Fill the hollowed-out centers of the 4 onion halves with the stuffing.

5. Lightly oil the base of your slow cooker pot, then place the stuffed onions into it. Carefully pour the stock around the onions, cover, and cook on high for 4 hours, basting the onions once.

6. Transfer the delicate onions to a Swiss roll pan or shallow roasting pan, then place under a preheated broiler for 2–3 minutes to brown.

SERVING SUGGESTION
Serve with a leaf salad or as an accompaniment to a roast dinner.

SERVES 4

PREP 15 MINS

SOAK 20 MINS

COOKING 1¾–2¼ HRS

SETTING LOW & HIGH

Risotto is always a popular standby and it does work with your slow cooker, albeit not quite as well as the stovetop method. But using a slow cooker means you don't have to stand at the stove stirring the rice for 20 minutes. Give it a shot—I think you'll be impressed.

Wild mushroom risotto

3¼ pints vegetable stock

1oz dried cèpes (porcini), soaked in hot water for 20 minutes

6 tbsp unsalted butter

1 tbsp olive oil

1 onion, finely chopped

1 celery stalk, finely chopped

1 garlic clove, finely chopped

1 carrot, finely chopped

1 thyme sprig

1 bay leaf

1¾ cups Arborio risotto rice

1 cup full-bodied red wine

3 cups fresh wild mushrooms, finely sliced

heaping ¾ freshly grated Parmesan

2 tbsp finely chopped flat-leaf parsley

to serve
green salad

1. Heat the stock in a pan and keep warm.

2. Strain the cèpes and reserve the soaking water. Finely chop the cèpes and set aside.

3. Melt half the butter with the oil in a heavy-based pan over medium heat. Add the onion, celery, garlic, carrot, thyme, and bay leaf and cook for about 6–8 minutes, stirring occasionally, until the onion has softened but not browned. Add the cèpes and cook for 3–4 minutes.

4. Add the rice and stir until the grains are well coated. Add the wine, mushroom-soaking liquid, and two-thirds of the stock. Bring to a boil and transfer to your slow cooker, then cover and cook on low for 1½–2 hours.

5. Add the fresh mushrooms, turn the slow cooker to high, cover, and cook for a further 15 minutes. Add more warm stock, if extra liquid is required to stop the risotto from drying out.

6. When the rice is cooked, fold in the remaining butter, the Parmesan, and parsley. Serve with a green salad.

SERVES 4 — PREP 15 MINS — COOKING 35 MINS — SETTING LOW & HIGH

Baked eggs have all but disappeared from domestic menus, although you occasionally see them in restaurants. They're very easy to prepare and produce a satisfying texture when cooked in the slow cooker.

Baked eggs with leeks and tomato

2 tbsp unsalted butter

½lb leeks, green discarded, white very thinly sliced

1 tsp soft thyme leaves

½ cup heavy cream

salt and freshly ground black pepper

½ cup Gruyère cheese, grated

4 large eggs

1 beefsteak tomato, cored and cut into 4 slices

2 tsp extra-virgin olive oil

to serve

crusty bread

1. Pour 1in boiling water into the bottom of your slow cooker, turn to high, and place an upturned plate or saucer in the bottom.

2. Grease 4 large individual ramekins with half the butter.

3. Melt the remaining butter in a skillet and, over medium heat, gently cook the leeks with the thyme for 5–8 minutes, stirring occasionally. Stir in half the cream, increase the heat, and cook for a further 2 minutes. Season to taste.

4. Spoon the leeks into the ramekins, pushing them slightly up the sides to create a hollow in the center. Sprinkle a little Gruyère over the leeks, then carefully break an egg into each hollow. Pour over the remaining cream and lightly season.

5. Gently place a slice of tomato over each egg, top with the remaining cheese, and drizzle with the oil. Place the ramekins in your slow cooker, cover, and cook on low for 30 minutes, until the whites are just setting.

6. Place the ramekins under a preheated broiler for 2–3 minutes until the cheese is browned.

7. Serve as an appetizer or supper dish with crusty bread.

SERVES
6–8

PREP
15 MINS +
REFRIGERATE
OVERNIGHT

COOKING
4 HRS

SETTING
HIGH

Here's something a little special for a dinner party. It requires a bit of patience, but for the keen cook it's worth the effort. Mix and match the smoked fish, for instance, using kippers instead of smoked haddock, and do make sure your loaf pan or terrine dish will fit inside your slow cooker.

Smoked fish terrine

1 tsp vegetable oil, for oiling

14oz best smoked salmon

1lb undyed smoked haddock, skinned

1lb hot-smoked salmon, skinned

2 eggs, lightly beaten

½ cup sour cream

2 tsp snipped chives

2 tsp extra-fine capers, drained

2 tsp finely chopped dill

2 tsp creamy horseradish sauce

salt and freshly ground black pepper

to serve

toast

1. Pour 1in warm water into the bottom of your slow cooker, turn it onto high, and place an upturned plate or saucer in the bottom.

2. Lightly oil a 2lb loaf pan or 9 x 5 x 3in terrine dish and line with plastic wrap, allowing a 3in overhang on each side.

3. Line the terrine with the smoked salmon slices, leaving a similar overhang to cover the top when the terrine is full.

4. Put the smoked haddock on a cutting board next to the terrine and cut to length to fill the loaf pan or terrine. Wrap this rectangle of smoked haddock in the remaining smoked salmon.

5. Cut the leftover smoked haddock into ½in chunks and place in a bowl. Flake the hot-smoked salmon into another bowl and set both aside.

6. In a third bowl, mix together the eggs, cream, chives, capers, dill, and horseradish sauce. Season well. Spoon half the mixture into the diced haddock, and the remaining half into the flaked salmon. Stir each of the mixtures to combine.

7. Spoon the smoked haddock mixture into the bottom of the terrine, top with the smoked-salmon-wrapped haddock, then finally top with the hot-smoked salmon mix. Level the surface and fold the overhanging smoked salmon over the top, then the overhanging plastic wrap. Seal well.

8. Place the terrine in the slow cooker. Carefully add more boiling water to come halfway up the sides of the terrine. Cover and cook on high for about 4 hours, until a skewer inserted in the terrine comes out clean.

9. Remove the terrine and place 2 or 3 cans on top to compress the filling. Leave to cool, then chill overnight in your fridge. Lift the terrine out of the mold with the help of the plastic wrap, then remove the plastic wrap and cut the terrine into thick slices. Serve with toast.

SERVES
4

PREP
30 MINS

COOKING
3–4 HRS

SETTING
HIGH

This is really nice presented at the table in its own wide-mouthed preserving jar. Cooking the terrine in the wire bail canning jar or a mason jar sterilizes it and so it will keep a lot longer than if you use a terrine mold or loaf pan.

Chicken, pork, apple, and walnut terrine

1 tbsp olive oil

1 onion, finely chopped

3 garlic cloves, crushed to a paste with a little sea salt

2 tsp soft thyme leaves

1 chicken breast, finely chopped

¾lb cleaned chicken livers, ¾ finely chopped and ¼ cut in half

2 slices smoked bacon, finely chopped

⅔lb ground pork

1 egg, beaten

3 tbsp Calvados or brandy

1 heaping cup fresh white breadcrumbs

3 pickled walnuts, drained and diced

2 tsp soft green peppercorns in brine, drained

1 tsp sea salt

1 all-purpose apple, peeled, cored, and diced

1. In a skillet, heat the olive oil and gently cook the onion, garlic, and thyme for 8 minutes, until softened but not colored. Allow to cool.

2. In a bowl, combine the chicken breast, finely chopped chicken livers, bacon, and ground pork. Beat together the egg and Calvados and add to the meat mixture with the onion and all the remaining ingredients, except the halved chicken livers. Stir well.

3. Divide half the meat mix between 2 x 2-cup sterilized canning jars. Press it down and top with the halved chicken livers, then the remaining meat mix, press it down again, and smooth the surface. Seal the lids and place the jars in your slow cooker, pour boiling water three-quarters of the way up the sides of the jars, cover, and cook on high for 3–4 hours until the meat is cooked and the juices are almost clear. Remove and cool.

4. Store in the fridge until ready to eat. Unopened, these terrines should last at least a couple of weeks.

SERVING SUGGESTION
Serve with hot country bread, cornichons, small chunks of Parmesan, and a little salad.

How to sterilize jars
See page 215 for details.

SERVES
4

PREP
20 MINS

COOKING
2¼ HRS

SETTING
HIGH

There aren't many dishes that win over most palates, but fish pie is one dish that does, whether it has a potato or pastry topping or, in this case, melting cheesy breadcrumbs.

A not-so-classic fish pie

½lb skinless, undyed smoked haddock,
  cut into bite-sized pieces

½lb skinless salmon,
  cut into bite-sized pieces

2 tbsp cornstarch

salt and freshly ground black pepper

¾ cup frozen petits pois, defrosted

¾ cup canned corn, drained

½ cup cream cheese

1 tbsp finely chopped dill

1 tsp English mustard powder

⅓ cup light cream

⅓ cup milk

1 tbsp creamy horseradish sauce

6oz cooked shrimp, shelled

½ cup fresh or dried white
  breadcrumbs

2 tbsp finely chopped flat-leaf parsley

1 tbsp olive oil

1 tsp sweet paprika

4 tbsp grated Parmesan

2 tsp snipped chives

½ cup Cheddar, grated

to serve

Salad of lettuce, tomato, and
  cucumber with hard-boiled eggs

1. Combine the haddock and salmon in a bowl and toss thoroughly with the cornstarch. Season. Mix with the peas and corn.

2. In another bowl, beat together the cream cheese, dill, mustard, cream, and milk. Fold in the horseradish sauce and the fish and vegetable mixture. Spoon into your slow cooker, cover, and cook on high for 2 hours.

3. Fold in the shrimp, cover, and cook on high for 10 minutes.

4. Meanwhile, in a food processor, blend together the breadcrumbs with the parsley, oil, paprika, Parmesan, and chives until the crumbs become pale green. Transfer to a bowl and combine with the Cheddar.

5. Remove the ceramic cooking pot from the slow cooker and sprinkle over the cheesy crumbs. Place under a preheated broiler for about 5 minutes until the topping is golden. Serve with a salad.

SERVES
4

PREP
45 MINS

COOKING
5½–6½
HRS

SETTING
LOW &
HIGH

Turkey is one of the healthy proteins, but it can be a bit bland. It never need be again, once you've tried this recipe. Although the ingredient list seems long, many of the ingredients are used in both parts of the recipe, so it's not as daunting as it first seems.

for the meatballs

1lb 2oz ground turkey

grated zest of 1 organic orange

4 ripe tomatoes, finely diced

2 garlic cloves, crushed to a paste

1 onion, coarsely grated

8 tbsp finely chopped flat-leaf parsley

1 tbsp finely chopped coriander leaves

1 heaping cup fresh white breadcrumbs

1 egg, lightly beaten

1 tbsp Worcestershire sauce

pinch of ground allspice

½ tsp each ground coriander and cumin

¼ tsp ground fennel

1 tbsp malt vinegar

3 tbsp grated Parmesan

½ tsp salt and ¼ tsp black pepper

1½ tbsp vegetable oil

for the pilaf

1½ tbsp vegetable oil

1 onion, coarsely grated

2 garlic cloves, crushed to a paste

pinch of freshly ground black pepper

pinch of ground allspice

½ tsp each ground coriander and cumin

¼ tsp ground fennel

2 carrots, finely chopped or grated

8oz can chopped tomatoes

3¼ cups chicken stock, boiling

1 heaping cup basmati rice, rinsed

4 cups baby spinach

½ bunch cilantro, roughly chopped

¼ cup cashews, chopped

2 tbsp red wine vinegar

½ bunch flat-leaf parsley, chopped

Turkey meatballs with tomato rice pilaf

1. To make the meatballs: in a bowl, combine the ground turkey, orange zest, tomatoes, garlic, onion, herbs, breadcrumbs, egg, Worcestershire sauce, spices, malt vinegar, and Parmesan.

2. Season with the salt and pepper, then mold into balls the size of a golf ball. Place a nonstick skillet over medium to high heat and add the oil. Brown the turkey balls on all sides. Remove to a plate and set aside.

3. To make the pilaf: heat the oil in the skillet, then add the onion and garlic and sweat them for 6–8 minutes. Add the spices and carrots and cook for 5 minutes, stirring occasionally. Pour in the chopped tomatoes and half the stock. Transfer to your slow cooker.

4. Add the meatballs to the sauce, cover, and cook on low for 4–5 hours until the meatballs are cooked through.

5. Add the remaining stock and the rice, stir to combine, turn the slow cooker to high, and cook, covered, for 40 minutes.

6. Lay the spinach and the cilantro on the surface and cook for 40 minutes, until the spinach has wilted. Stir to combine, then fold in the cashews and the red wine vinegar. Season to taste. Serve sprinkled with the parsley and with a green salad or broccoli, peas, or beans.

Slow cooker tips
Try these meatballs with your favorite tomato sauce recipe. Just add to the slow cooker, cover, and cook on low for 4–5 hours, until the meat has finished cooking.

If you make the pilaf on its own, cook it on high for 1½–2 hours.

Who can resist a traditional steak and kidney pudding? It came top in a recent BBC poll of Britain's best-loved dishes. The beauty of this dish is the fact that you can change the filling, for instance, by reducing the quantity of meat and adding more vegetables.

Steak and kidney pudding

1½lb chuck steak or blade steak,
   cut into 1in cubes
½lb ox kidney, cut into 1in cubes
2 small onions, finely chopped
large pinch of celery salt
1 tsp soft thyme leaves
salt and freshly ground black pepper
⅔ cup fresh beef stock
   (store-bought is fine)
1 tsp English mustard powder
1 tbsp tomato paste
1 tbsp Worcestershire sauce
unsalted butter, for greasing
2 tbsp all-purpose flour

1¼ cups self-rising flour, plus
   extra for dusting
½ tsp salt
7oz shredded beef suet
freshly ground black pepper

to serve
mashed potatoes
buttered peas

1. Place the steak and kidney in a large bowl. Stir in the onion, celery salt, thyme, and seasoning. Toss together lightly and set to one side, or cover with plastic wrap and chill for up to 24 hours to allow the flavors to develop.

2. Meanwhile, mix together the stock, tomato paste, and Worcestershire sauce. Butter a 7½in pudding basin.

3. To make the suet pastry: sift the flour and salt into a large bowl. Add the suet and season with pepper. Lightly mix and add 1¼ cups cold water, a little at a time, cutting through the dough with a round-bladed knife. Use your hands to form the soft pastry.

4. Roll out on a lightly floured worktop into a round disk roughly ½in thick. Cut out a wedge (one-quarter) of the pastry to within 1in of the center and set aside. Lift the remaining pastry into the basin and overlap the cut edges. Dampen the edges with a little water and press together, so that the basin is completely lined. Leave at least ½in overhanging the rim.

5. Add the flour to the steak and kidney mixture and stir gently to combine. Place batches of the meat mixture into a sieve (over a bowl) and shake to remove any excess flour. Spoon into the lined basin, being careful not to press it down, then pour in enough beef stock mixture to come nearly two-thirds up to the top of the basin, but not covering the meat completely.

6. Roll out the reserved pastry into a circle 1in larger than the top of the basin and ½in thick. Dampen the edges of the pastry lining the basin, place the lid over the filling, and press the 2 edges together to seal. Trim off any excess pastry and make 2 small slits in the center of the lid.

7. Cover with a double layer of buttered foil, pleated in the center to allow for expansion. Secure the foil with twine, making a handle to lift the basin. Place on an upturned plate in the slow cooker and pour in boiling water to come two-thirds of the way up the side of the basin. Cover and cook on high for 6 hours until cooked, topping up with boiling water occasionally.

8. Cut the twine and remove the foil. Serve with mashed potatoes and buttered peas.

Stews

A stew of fish in a saffron broth

see page 122

This adds a little flavor of the Mediterranean to your menu.
It's great as a vegetarian dish on its own or as an accompaniment
to fish, poultry, or meat.

Italian leek stew

1 tbsp olive oil

2¼lb leeks, cut into 1¼in chunks
and washed

1 onion, finely chopped

2 garlic cloves, finely chopped

½ tsp cayenne pepper

⅓ cup Kalamata olives, pitted and
roughly chopped

14oz can chopped tomatoes

14oz can cranberry beans, drained
and rinsed

8oz-ball mozzarella, finely diced

12 large basil leaves, torn into small
pieces

salt and freshly ground black pepper

to serve
brown rice

1. Heat the oil in a large skillet over medium heat and add the leeks, onion, garlic, and cayenne. Fry, stirring occasionally, until lightly browned. Transfer to your slow cooker.

2. Add the olives and tomatoes, plus ¾ cup water and the beans, then stir to combine. Cook on low for 5–6 hours.

3. Turn the slow cooker to high and stir in the mozzarella and basil. Cover and cook for a further 15 minutes.

4. Season to taste and serve with brown rice.

Slow cooker tips
You can cook this for up to 8 hours before the leeks become past their best.

SERVES
4

PREP
15 MINS

COOKING
6–8 HRS

SETTING
LOW

**This is based loosely on mushrooms à la grecque: it's delicious as part
of a meze, as a vegetarian dish served with couscous or rice, or even as a
vegetable with grilled or roast meats.**

Button mushroom and tomato stew

1lb button mushrooms

juice and grated zest of 1 unwaxed or
   organic lemon

2 tbsp olive oil

3 garlic cloves, crushed to a paste with
   a little sea salt

4–5 shallots, finely chopped

1 tbsp coriander seeds

1 tbsp fennel seeds

1 bay leaf

14oz can chopped tomatoes

1 large glass dry white wine

1 red chile

1 tbsp tomato paste

1 tbsp superfine sugar

salt and freshly ground black pepper

to garnish
1 tbsp finely chopped flat-leaf parsley

to serve
basmati rice or penne pasta
plain, strained yogurt

1. Toss the mushrooms with the lemon juice and zest in a bowl.

2. In a deep skillet, heat a generous glug of the olive oil, add the garlic and shallots, and cook them gently for 8–10 minutes. Transfer them to your slow cooker.

3. Add the remaining ingredients, except the parsley, stir to combine, cover, and cook on low for 6–8 hours.

4. Season to taste and garnish with the parsley.

SERVING SUGGESTION
For a simple lunch, this is good with basmati rice or penne pasta. It's excellent with a dollop of plain, strained yogurt too.

SERVES
4

PREP
15 MINS

COOKING
2 HRS

SETTING
LOW &
HIGH

Not many of us think about treating fish in the same manner as a piece of meat, but if you use a robust fish, such as a yellowfin tuna, salmon, or even mackerel, you will find this recipe works like a dream.

Fillets of fish in a smoky barbecue sauce

4 x 7oz firm fish fillets
salt and freshly ground black pepper

for the barbecue sauce
1 tbsp canola or vegetable oil
1 onion, finely chopped
2 garlic cloves, crushed to a paste with
   a little sea salt
2 tsp fennel seeds
1 tsp chili powder
2 tsp smoked paprika
1 tbsp soy sauce
2 tbsp soft dark brown sugar
2 tbsp sherry vinegar
2 tbsp mustard
$^2/_3$ cup good tomato ketchup

to serve
potato wedges

1. Heat the oil in a skillet and cook the onion and garlic gently over low heat for 8–10 minutes, until the onions have softened but not colored.

2. Stir in the fennel seeds, chili powder, paprika, soy sauce, sugar, vinegar, mustard, and ketchup. Heat slowly until boiling, then carefully pour into your slow cooker.

3. Cover and cook the barbecue sauce on low for 1 hour, then increase to high, add the fish fillets, and push under the surface of the sauce. Cover and cook for 1 hour, until the fish is tender and cooked.

4. Season to taste. Serve with fried or oven-baked potato wedges.

Also try
Do try cooking chicken thighs, instead of the fish, in this sauce. Add the chicken to the sauce in the slow cooker at the end of step 2, cover, and cook on low for 6–8 hours until the meat is thoroughly cooked.

SERVES
6

PREP
10 MINS

COOKING
4¼ HRS

SETTING
**LOW &
HIGH**

I love a good soupy fish stew and this one is a favorite. Fear not that the fish selection is too onerous. Just remember the three types of fish and their cooking times and the recipe is immediately simplified: squid and octopus for at least 4 hours on low; fish 1¼–1½ hours on low; shellfish 15–20 minutes on high.

A stew of fish in a saffron broth

2 pints dashi or fish stock

pinch of saffron strands

4 tbsp each olive oil and sesame oil

2 shallots, finely diced

2 garlic cloves, crushed to a paste with a little sea salt

2 tbsp roughly chopped cilantro root or stems

2in piece of fresh ginger, grated

2 red chiles, seeded and diced

1¼ cups dry white wine

2 bay leaves

2 dried strips of orange peel

2lb baby squid, cleaned

½lb monkfish fillet, cut into 1in dice

¼lb red mullet fillets (left whole)

2lb small mussels

2lb small clams

1¼ cups sugar snap peas, topped and tailed

8 scallions, cut into 1in pieces

1 scallions, thinly sliced

8 cherry tomatoes, halved

salt and freshly ground black pepper

to serve

crusty bread

salad of Baby Gem or Romaine lettuce

1. Place the dashi or stock and saffron in a bowl to infuse for 15 minutes.

2. Heat the oils in a large skillet, add the shallots, garlic, cilantro root, ginger, and chiles and cook for about 6 minutes, until softened but not browned. Spoon into your slow cooker, then add the white wine, bay leaves, orange peel, squid, and saffron broth. Cover and cook on low for 2½ hours, then add the monkfish and mullet, cover again, and cook on low for a further 1¼ hours.

3. Meanwhile, clean the mussels and clams, discarding any that do not close when tapped against the sink.

4. Turn the slow cooker to high and add the mussels, clams, sugar snap peas, scallions, zucchini, and cherry tomatoes. Cook for a further 20 minutes. Discard any mussels or clams that haven't opened. Season the stew to taste.

5. Pour into a large, warm soup tureen and serve with crusty bread and a large bowl of salad.

Choosing fish
Try to buy sustainably caught fish wherever possible.

The Spanish love fish and consequently it fetches a much higher price in their markets than fish does in other countries. I'm never sure why we don't eat more fish here in the UK. After all, we do live on an island. On average we eat less than one portion per week and then wonder why we're not a particularly healthy population.

A robust Spanish fish and red pepper stew

3 tbsp good olive oil

2 onions, finely chopped

4 garlic cloves, crushed to a paste with a little sea salt

1 tbsp harissa paste

⅓ cup dry white wine

14oz can chopped tomatoes

2 bay leaves

¼ tsp dried red pepper flakes

1½ tsp sweet paprika

1lb potatoes, cut into 2in dice

1 fennel bulb, tough outer layer removed, roughly chopped

1 red pepper, seeded and cut into 1in pieces

1 yellow pepper, cored, seeded, and cut into 1in pieces

¾lb line-caught tuna, cut into 1in pieces

¾lb hake or cod, cut into 1in pieces

salt and freshly ground black pepper

to serve

crusty bread

1. Heat the olive oil in a saucepan, add the onions and garlic, and cook gently for 8–10 minutes until the onions have softened but not colored. Add the harissa, white wine, tomatoes, bay leaves, red pepper flakes, and paprika, and bring slowly to a boil. Pour carefully into the slow cooker.

2. Add the potatoes, fennel, and peppers, stir to combine, then cover and cook on low for 4–6 hours, until the potatoes are tender.

3. Turn the slow cooker to high and stir in the fish pieces. Cover and cook for 30 minutes until the fish is cooked.

4. Season to taste and serve with crusty bread.

SERVES
4

PREP
45 MINS

COOKING
6–8 HRS

SETTING
LOW

Forget the days of thrashing octopus on the rocks to tenderize it—a few days in the freezer works just as well.

Greek octopus stew

2¼lb octopus, cleaned, frozen for 3 days, and defrosted

3 tbsp olive oil

2 large Spanish onions, roughly chopped

6 garlic cloves, finely chopped

2 bay leaves

1 tsp finely chopped oregano leaves

1 cinnamon stick

4 cloves

¾ cup golden raisins

6 grinds of freshly ground black pepper

heaping ¾ cup pine nuts, toasted

1 tbsp tomato paste

1 tbsp anchovy essence

¾ cup dry red wine

⅓ cup *Punt e Mes* or red vermouth

3 tbsp extra-virgin olive oil

salt and freshly ground black pepper

to serve

long-grain rice

pappardelle

1. Put the octopus in a saucepan and cover with cold water. Bring to a boil and simmer for 30 minutes. Drain and wash thoroughly in cold water. Cut the octopus into bite-sized pieces and set aside.

2. Put the olive oil in a skillet over medium heat. Add the onion, garlic, bay leaves, and oregano and cook for 10 minutes, until the onion has softened but not colored.

3. Transfer to your slow cooker and add the octopus, cinnamon, cloves, golden raisins, black pepper, pine nuts, tomato paste, and anchovy essence, then stir to combine. Add ¾ cup water, red wine, *Punt e Mes*, and extra-virgin olive oil. Cover and cook on low for 6–8 hours until the octopus is cooked and tender.

4. If you want the sauce to be thicker, strain the stew through a colander placed over a large bowl. Place the octopus mixture in a warm bowl and cover with foil to keep warm. Transfer the strained sauce to a saucepan and boil vigorously, until reduced to your liking. Season to taste, return the octopus mixture to the pan, and stir to combine.

5. Serve with rice or pappardelle.

SERVES
4–6

PREP
20 MINS

COOKING
6½–7½ HRS

SETTING
LOW & HIGH

Rabbit has faded in popularity over the years, which is a shame because it has much more flavor that most chickens. But who am I to say? If you prefer chicken, then go for it: I would use drumsticks in this recipe.

Rabbit with fennel, peppers, and Belgian endive

4 tbsp extra-virgin olive oil

1 medium onion, finely chopped

1 tsp finely chopped rosemary leaves

2 garlic cloves, finely diced

1 bay leaf

1 large head of fennel, tough outer layer removed and cut into 8 wedges through the root end

2 Belgian endive, halved lengthways

1 large red pepper, roasted, peeled, and cut into 6 lengthways, seeds discarded

1 large orange pepper, roasted, peeled, and cut into 6 lengthways, seeds discarded

1 tsp dried red pepper flakes

2¼lb rabbit pieces on the bone

2 cups chicken stock

¾ cup frozen peas, defrosted

1 tbsp finely chopped mint

2 tbsp coarsely chopped flat-leaf parsley

to serve
creamy mashed potatoes

1. Heat the oil in a skillet over medium heat and cook the onion, rosemary, garlic, and bay leaf for about 8 minutes, until the onions are soft and translucent. Add the fennel wedges and the Belgian endive and cook for a further 8 minutes, turning gently, until the fennel and endive have taken on a little color. Transfer to the slow cooker.

2. Add the peppers, red pepper flakes, rabbit, and stock. Stir to combine. Cover with the lid and cook on slow for 6–7 hours until the meat is cooked.

3. Increase the heat to high and add the peas, mint, and parsley. Stir to combine and then cook, uncovered, for 20 minutes.

4. Serve with creamy mashed potatoes.

Also try
You could also cook hare pieces or diced venison or venison medallion steaks using the same cooking times.

SERVES
4

PREP
40 MINS

MARINATE
2 HRS

COOKING
1 HR

HOB

Rabbit can have a tendency to be dry so gentle cooking is crucial either in a covered pan on the stove or gently bubbling in a slow cooker. Flavored here with pancetta, garlic, allspice, and wine, this dish tells a story of rural Italian cooking.

Rabbit with rosemary

½ cup olive oil

2 leeks, finely chopped

2 carrots, finely chopped

2 celery stalks, finely chopped

2 bay leaves

4 dried red chiles

3¼lb rabbit, jointed, or
   8 hind legs, sinews removed

salt and freshly ground black pepper

6oz pancetta, diced, or smoked bacon,
   cut into lardons

6 garlic cloves, peeled

1 tsp ground allspice

2 tbsp all-purpose flour

2 cups red wine

1¼ cup fresh chicken stock
   (store-bought is fine)

2 tbsp finely chopped rosemary leaves

to serve

mashed potatoes or pappardelle

buttered peas (optional)

1. Place the olive oil, leeks, carrots, celery, bay leaves, and chiles in a nonmetallic bowl. Add the rabbit and season generously, then stir to combine. Cover with plastic wrap and leave to marinate in the fridge for at least 2 hours but ideally for 24 hours, stirring a couple of times.

2. Put a large Dutch oven over high heat. Remove the rabbit from the marinade, brushing off the vegetables, and add to the pot in batches. Fry for about 10 minutes until nicely browned all over, turning regularly. Transfer to a plate.

3. Remove the bay leaves from the marinade and reserve, then remove and discard the chiles. Add the pancetta to the Dutch oven and cook for 6–8 minutes to release the fat, then add the marinated vegetable mixture, and the garlic. Cook for about 10 minutes over medium heat, stirring occasionally, until the vegetables are lightly golden and just tender.

4. Stir the allspice and flour into the pot and cook for 1–2 minutes, being careful not to let the flour catch on the bottom. Gradually pour in the wine, stirring constantly, then turn up the heat and boil for a few moments.

5. Pour in the stock and stir to combine, then turn down the heat and add the browned rabbit pieces, reserved bay leaves, and the rosemary. Cover and simmer for about 45 minutes, until the rabbit is cooked and completely tender. Season to taste.

6. Serve straight from the Dutch oven with bowls of mashed potato or pappardelle, and buttered peas, if you like.

To make this in a slow cooker
At step 5, instead of simmering the stew on the stove, you can transfer it to a slow cooker, cover, and cook for 6–8 hours on low, until the rabbit is cooked.

I love pork. I love the flavor pork fat gives to a stew. This is real country fare—no airs or graces, towers or foams, just good honest cooking.

Duck stew with white beans

2 tbsp duck fat

2 onions, finely diced

1 carrot, finely diced

1 celery stick, finely diced

8 garlic cloves, peeled

2 tsp tomato paste

14oz can chopped tomatoes

¾ cup Martini Extra Dry

2 x 14oz cans cannellini beans, drained and rinsed

½lb rind from the salt pork, cut into ¼in dice (optional)

½lb salt pork, blanched in boiling water for 10 minutes, drained and cut into lardons

2 thyme sprigs

2 bay leaves

2 cups chicken stock or water

4 duck confit legs, skin removed, meat shredded or diced

salt and freshly ground white pepper

to serve

buttered cabbage or spinach

crusty bread

1. Melt the duck fat in a skillet over medium heat, then fry the onions, carrot, celery, and garlic for 6–8 minutes, until golden brown. Mash the garlic cloves with the back of a fork. Add the tomato paste, tomatoes, and Martini, stir to combine, then transfer to your slow cooker.

2. Mix in the beans, diced salt pork rind, if using, salt pork lardons, thyme, and bay leaves. Add the chicken stock, cover, and cook on low for 6 hours, until the meat is cooked.

3. Turn the slow cooker to high, add the duck, and cook for 20 minutes.

4. Season to taste. Serve with buttered cabbage or spinach and crusty fresh bread.

SERVES
4

PREP
20 MINS

COOKING
6¼–7¼ HRS

SETTING
LOW & HIGH

This is a good, old-fashioned chicken stew with a creamy finish. You can use rabbit or pork and a host of root vegetables, if you wish, in a fricassee. But here, I've stuck with tradition, using just baby onions and button mushrooms, and tomatoes to garnish.

Chicken, mushroom, and onion fricassee

2 tbsp vegetable oil
8 chicken thighs, skin on
2 tbsp unsalted butter
24 pickling onions, peeled
2 garlic cloves, finely chopped
½lb button mushrooms
3 tbsp all-purpose flour
1 tsp sweet paprika
¾ cup dry white wine
2½ cups good chicken stock, boiling
1 thyme sprig
1 bay leaf
½ cup heavy cream
2 tomatoes, seeded and diced
4 tbsp finely chopped flat-leaf parsley
1 tsp finely chopped tarragon
salt and freshly ground black pepper

to serve
green vegetable
new potatoes

1. Put the oil in a large skillet over high heat and fry the chicken thighs until golden all over. Remove and set aside.

2. Add the butter to the same pan, lower the heat to medium, and cook the onions, garlic, and mushrooms until golden—you may have to do this in batches—then set aside.

3. Add the flour and paprika to the fat in the skillet and stir to combine. Cook gently for 3 minutes, until the roux is lightly browned.

4. Pour in the wine and stir vigorously, loosening any pieces stuck to the bottom of the skillet, until emulsified. Slowly add a ladleful of stock at a time, whisking between each addition, and bring to a simmer. Pour into your slow cooker pot.

5. Fold in the onions and mushrooms, chicken, thyme, and bay leaf. Cover and cook on low for 6–7 hours, until the chicken is thoroughly cooked.

6. Using a slotted spoon, remove the chicken and vegetables to a warm dish, cover loosely in foil, and set aside.

7. To make the sauce in the slow cooker, fold in the heavy cream, tomatoes, parsley, and tarragon, cover, and cook on high for 15 minutes. Season to taste.

8. Pour the sauce over the chicken and vegetables, and serve with your favorite green vegetable and new potatoes.

Also try
Try this dish with rabbit hind legs or pork shoulder.

SERVES
4

PREP
45 MINS

COOKING
8 HRS

SETTING
LOW &
HIGH

This is a great casserole for a cold day with a real depth of flavor provided by the fruit. You can substitute beef for the venison, if you prefer. I'm sure that once you've tried this recipe it will become one of your one-bowl favorites.

2¼lb stewing venison, cut into 1¼in cubes

4 tbsp seasoned flour

2 tbsp vegetable oil or beef dripping

6oz smoked bacon, diced

2 celery stalks, finely chopped

1 large onion, finely chopped

2 garlic cloves, finely chopped

2 thyme sprigs

2 tbsp redcurrant jelly

¾ cup red wine

2 cups game or beef stock

⅓ cup port

1 tbsp Worcestershire sauce

12 pitted prunes

½ cup dried cherries

½ cup dried cranberries

7oz chestnuts, precooked and peeled

¼lb button mushrooms

2 bay leaves

grated zest of 1 organic orange

1 tbsp tomato paste

handful flat-leaf parsley, chopped

for the dumplings

1 heaping cup all-purpose flour

1 tsp salt

½ heaping tsp baking powder

3oz shredded beef suet

1 tbsp olive oil

2 tsp creamy horseradish sauce

3 tsp finely chopped flat-leaf parsley

3 tbsp snipped chives

½ cup milk

melted butter, for brushing

Winter venison in a bowl with herb dumplings

1. Toss the venison in the seasoned flour (see Antony's Tips page 86).

2. Put the oil in a skillet over high heat and brown the venison all over—you may need to do this in batches. Remove with a slotted spoon and set aside.

3. In the same skillet, add the bacon, celery, onion, garlic, and thyme, then soften over medium heat for 8–10 minutes without browning. Transfer to a bowl with the venison, add the remaining casserole ingredients, except the parsley, and toss to combine. Transfer to your slow cooker, cover, and cook on low for 7 hours, until the meat is cooked.

4. Meanwhile, 1½ hours before the end of the cooking time, make the dumplings. Sift the flour, salt, and baking powder into a large bowl. Add the suet. Make a well in the center and add the olive oil, horseradish, and herbs, pour in a little of the milk, then mix with a fork to form a soft dough, adding more milk as necessary. Place the dough on a lightly floured surface and knead for 2 minutes. Divide and shape into 12 dumplings.

5. After 7 hours, turn up the slow cooker to high. Season the casserole with pepper and stir to combine. Brush each dumpling with a little melted butter and then place on the surface of the casserole. Cover and cook for 50–60 minutes, until the dumplings have risen.

6. Allow to rest for 5 minutes, then skim off any fat that has risen to the surface. To serve, sprinkle with the parsley.

Chickpeas are often part of a vegetarian's staple diet, but they are also a great addition to meat stews because they are a great vehicle for delicious flavors. Feel free to add more vegetables to the lamb, especially green ones, toward the end of the cooking time.

Pot-roasted lamb with chickpeas, sweet potatoes, and spices

1¾lb boneless leg of lamb,
  cut into 1in dice

salt

2 tbsp vegetable oil

2 sweet potatoes, cut into 1in chunks

14oz can whole tomatoes

14oz can chickpeas, drained and rinsed

2 cups lamb or chicken stock

3–4 tsp garam masala

2 handfuls spinach

¾ cup frozen peas, defrosted

for the marinade

3 tsp ground turmeric

2 tsp chili powder

2 tsp ground cumin

2 tbsp ground coriander

2 bay leaves

4–6 medium-sized hot green chiles

3 medium onions, finely chopped

6–8 garlic cloves, finely chopped

½in piece of fresh ginger,
  finely chopped

3 tbsp mustard oil

1 tsp superfine sugar

to serve

basmati rice

1. Mix the lamb with all the marinade ingredients in a large bowl. Add a little salt to taste. Cover with plastic wrap and leave for at least 2 hours at room temperature to marinate (or for 24 hours in the fridge).

2. In a large Dutch oven, heat the vegetable oil to smoking, reduce the heat to medium, then add the meat and all the marinade ingredients. Stir-fry for 12–15 minutes until brown all over but not scorched. Transfer the mixture to your slow cooker.

3. Add the sweet potatoes, tomatoes, chickpeas, and stock. Stir to mix well. Cover and cook on low for 7–8 hours, until the meat is cooked.

4. Stir in the garam masala, spinach, and peas, turn to high, and cook, uncovered, for 20 minutes. Serve with steamed basmati rice.

SERVES
4

PREP
15 MINS

COOKING
2½ HRS

OVEN

We tend to forget old classics, but not many dishes can touch the flavors of a Lancashire hotpot. Don't be turned off by the idea of using lamb shoulder blade chops with the bone in. After the long, slow cooking, the meat is so meltingly soft it can be easily pulled away from the bones using a fork.

Lancashire hotpot

2¼lb lamb shoulder blade chops, bone-in

4 lamb kidneys, skinned, halved horizontally, and the core (the fatty, white half-moon inside) removed

salt and freshly ground black pepper

1 tbsp vegetable oil

4 tbsp unsalted butter

2¼lb potatoes, peeled and cut into thick slices

3 onions, finely sliced

2 thyme sprigs

2 bay leaves

1 tbsp superfine sugar

2 cups lamb stock

1. Preheat the oven to 325°F. Season all the chops and kidneys with salt and plenty of pepper. Heat the oil in a skillet over high heat and brown the chops and kidneys all over, then set aside.

2. Butter the bottom of a heavy-based casserole dish with 1 tbsp of the butter.

3. Place an overlapping layer of potatoes in the bottom of the casserole. Top this with the chops, kidney halves, and onions. Tuck in the thyme sprigs and bay leaves. Season with extra salt and pepper and add the sugar.

4. Finish with the remaining potato slices, slightly overlapping each slice. Pour in the stock carefully so that it doesn't cover the top layer of potato.

5. Melt the remaining butter and brush the top of the potatoes with it. Cover the casserole with a lid and cook in the oven for 2 hours, then remove the lid, increase the heat to 400°F, and cook for a further 30 minutes or until the potatoes are golden brown and the meat cooked.

SERVING SUGGESTION
This is a one-pot meal, but traditionally you might serve it with pickled red cabbage on the side.

To make this in a slow cooker
If you would prefer to use your slow cooker, you can cook this for 8–10 hours on low, then brown under a hot broiler. Make sure the stock is boiling hot when you add it and that your slow cooker is large enough.

SERVES
6–8

PREP
30 MINS

MARINATE
OVER-
NIGHT

COOKING
4 HRS

OVEN

Transform ordinary chuck or blade steak into this classic French casserole. Begin by marinating the night before you need it in a mixture of red burgundy, thyme, and garlic then slowly cook it so that the beef becomes incredibly tender, moist, and full of flavor.

Beef bourguignon

4 tbsp olive oil

1 large carrot, cut into chunks

1 large onion, cut into chunks

2 celery stalks, roughly chopped

1 bottle red Burgundy

2 thyme sprigs

1 head of garlic, cut in half horizontally

4 bay leaves

3lb 5oz chuck steak or blade steak,
    cut into 2in cubes

2 tbsp unsalted butter

8oz smoked bacon or pancetta,
    cut into lardons

1lb shallots, peeled

2 tbsp plain flour

2½ cups fresh beef stock (store-bought
    is fine)

salt and freshly ground black pepper

¾lb small cremino mushrooms,
    trimmed

5 tbsp brandy

to garnish

roughly chopped flat-leaf parsley

to serve

broccoli

1. Put 1 tbsp oil in a heavy-based pan over medium heat. Add the carrot, onion, and celery and cook for 2–3 minutes, stirring. Pour in the wine and stir in the thyme, garlic, and 2 bay leaves. Bring to a boil, then reduce the heat and simmer, uncovered, for 15 minutes. Allow to cool completely.

2. Place the beef in a large nonmetallic bowl and pour over the wine mixture. Cover with plastic wrap and marinate overnight in the fridge.

3. Preheat the oven to 300°F. Place a colander over a large bowl, then strain the beef. Reserve the liquid marinade and set aside. Put 1 tbsp of the butter and 1 tbsp oil in a large skillet over medium heat. Add the bacon and cook for 6–8 minutes, stirring occasionally, until sizzling and golden brown. Stir in the shallots and then transfer to a large casserole dish with a lid.

4. Put 1 tbsp oil in the same skillet over high heat. Pat dry the drained beef cubes with paper towels. Brown all over, in batches. Remove with a slotted spoon and transfer to the casserole dish with the bacon and shallots.

5. Add 2–3 large spoonfuls of the reserved marinade to the skillet and allow to bubble, scraping the bottom of the skillet with a wooden spoon to loosen any sediment. Pour into the casserole dish. Sprinkle over the flour and stir in the remaining marinade and bay leaves and stock. Season generously and bring to a boil, then cover and place in the oven for 3–3½ hours, until the beef is cooked and very tender but still holding its shape.

6. About 50 minutes before the end of the cooking time, heat the remaining oil and butter in a skillet and cook the mushrooms for 6–8 minutes until lightly browned. Add the brandy and cook for another few minutes, then stir into the casserole dish, replace the lid, and return it to the oven for 30 minutes.

7. Remove the casserole from the oven and season to taste. Sprinkle with the parsley and serve with a bowl of steamed broccoli.

To make this in a slow cooker
Make sure your slow cooker is large enough to hold all the ingredients. You will need to reduce both the wine and stock by about one-third. Transfer the beef bourguignon to your slow cooker in step 5, once it is boiling. Cover and cook for on low for 6–8 hours until the meat is cooked. Add the mushroom mixture prepared in step 6 for the last hour of cooking.

SERVES
4–6

PREP
30 MINS

COOKING
2 HRS

STOVE

This is one of our best-selling dishes at The Greyhound. I add red peppers and gherkins to the traditional recipe, which I think enhance this classic. If you get a little delayed, don't worry, an extra half an hour or so will be fine—that's the beauty of slow cooking. Just add a little stock if needed, before you stir in the sour cream.

Paprika goulash

1½lb onions, roughly chopped

2 tbsp unsalted butter

2¼lb chuck steak or brisket, cut into 1½in cubes

¼ cup seasoned all-purpose flour (see page 86)

¼lb salt pork or smoked bacon, cut into ½in cubes

3 garlic cloves, finely chopped

1 red pepper, cored, seeded, and cut into ½in dice

2 tsp caraway seeds

2 tsp sweet paprika, plus extra for serving

2½ cups beef stock

2 tbsp tomato paste

1 tsp sea salt

freshly ground black pepper

1¼ cups sour cream

2 tbsp chopped sour gherkins or cornichons

to serve

new potatoes

sour cream, mixed with chopped sour gherkins or cornichons

1. Put the onions in a food processor and blitz to a purée. Set aside.

2. Melt the butter in a heavy-based pan. Roll the beef in the seasoned flour, turn the heat under the pan to high, and fry in the butter until golden on all sides. Remove with a slotted spoon and set aside.

3. Add the salt pork to the same saucepan and brown all over, then add the garlic, red pepper, onion purée, caraway, and paprika and cook over medium heat for 3 minutes, stirring occasionally.

4. Return the beef to the pan and add the stock, tomato paste, salt, and a few grindings of black pepper. Bring to a boil, reduce the heat, cover, and then simmer for 2 hours, stirring occasionally, until the meat is cooked.

5. Five minutes before the end of cooking, stir in the sour cream with the gherkins but do not allow to reboil. Serve with new potatoes, with dollops of more sour cream mixed with chopped gherkins, and sprinkled with a little more paprika.

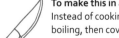

To make this in a slow cooker
Instead of cooking the goulash on the stove in step 4, transfer the mixture to the slow cooker when boiling, then cover and cook on low for 6–8 hours until the meat is cooked. Continue with step 5.

SERVES
4

PREP
30 MINS

COOKING
8–10 HRS

SETTING
**HIGH &
LOW**

**I'm cheating a little here, and why not? It takes a couple of days to make
proper cassoulet, including all the stages. So this is not the real McCoy,
but it's delicious all the same.**

Cassoulet in a day

4 duck legs

½lb salt pork, cut into 1in chunks

1 onion, roughly chopped

½lb smoked Toulouse sausages,
  thickly sliced, or raw garlic sausage,
  skin removed, cut into 1in chunks

2 celery stalks, thinly sliced

4 garlic cloves, finely chopped

2 tbsp all-purpose flour

14oz can chopped tomatoes

2 tbsp tomato paste

3 thyme sprigs

2 bay leaves

½ tsp ground cloves

¾ cup dry white wine

1 cup chicken stock

salt and freshly ground black pepper

2 x 14oz cans navy beans, great
  Northern beans, or cannellini beans,
  drained and rinsed

1 cup fresh white breadcrumbs

to serve

green salad

crusty bread

1. Trim any excess fat from the duck legs and discard, then dry-fry in a large
skillet over low heat until the fat begins to run. Increase the heat and brown
the legs all over. Lift out and set aside. Add the diced salt pork and onion
and fry until lightly browned.

2. Stir in the sausage, celery, and garlic, fry for 2 minutes, then mix in the
flour, tomatoes, tomato paste, herbs, and cloves. Add the wine and stock
and bring to a boil. Season well.

3. Transfer half the beans to the slow cooker. Add half the hot tomato
mixture, then arrange the duck over the top in a single layer. Cover with the
remaining beans and spread the remaining tomato mixture in an even layer
on top, then sprinkle with the breadcrumbs.

4. Cover and cook on high for 30 minutes, reduce the heat to low, and cook
for 7½–9½ hours, until the breadcrumbs have absorbed the sauce and the
duck is cooked and almost falls off the bone when tested with a spoon.

5. Ladle into 4 warm shallow soup bowls.

SERVING SUGGESTION
A large bowl of salad and some crusty bread is all you need to accompany
this. Try tossing a few handfuls of watercress leaves, some dandelion, or
arugula, and some separated leaves of red-tinged Belgian endive with a
dressing of olive oil and sherry vinegar.

SERVES
4

PREP
50 MINS

COOKING
7–8 HRS

SETTING
LOW

I think many people equate meatballs with a cheap meal, but why not make the most of them? I've gone down the Italian route, packing them with loads of flavor and accompanying them with a yummy tomato sauce.

for the meatballs

1 slice of white bread

¼ cup milk

1lb 2oz ground pork

1 apple, peeled, cored, and grated

3 scallions, finely chopped

¼ cup Kalamata olives, pitted and roughly chopped

scant ½ cup grated Parmesan

1 tbsp finely chopped lemon thyme leaves (or thyme or oregano)

1 tbsp clear honey

1 egg, beaten

1 garlic clove, crushed to a paste with a little sea salt

salt and freshly ground black pepper

1 tbsp olive oil

for the sauce

1 garlic clove, crushed to a paste with a little sea salt

1 red chile, finely chopped

2 anchovy fillets in oil, chopped

1 onion, finely chopped

2 x 14oz cans chopped tomatoes

4 thyme sprigs

1 tbsp superfine sugar

to serve

buttered fettuccine

grated zest of ½ unwaxed lemon

¼ cup grated Parmesan

small basil leaves

Pork, apple, and lemon thyme meatballs

1. Tear the bread into small pieces and soak it in the milk for 5 minutes. Squeeze some of the milk from the bread, then place the bread in the bowl with the remaining meatball ingredients. Mix well, season, and then shape into balls the size of golf balls.

2. Put the oil in a large skillet over high heat, then fry the meatballs until brown all over. Remove to a plate and set aside.

3. Add the garlic, chile, anchovy, and onion to the skillet and fry over gentle heat for about 8 minutes to soften but not color. Add the tomatoes, thyme, and sugar, and simmer for 10 minutes, then season. Spoon the sauce into your slow cooker, then add the meatballs, toss gently to combine, cover, and cook on low for 7–8 hours until the meatballs are cooked.

4. Serve on buttered fettuccine, and sprinkle with lemon zest, grated Parmesan, and basil leaves.

To prepare in advance
You can make the meatballs in advance to save time. Refrigerate overnight and then fry them in the morning before going to work.

SERVES

PREP
25 MINS

SOAK
30 MINS

COOKING
7¼–10¼
HRS

SETTING
**LOW &
HIGH**

**In the Deep South they love big flavors and their version of paella lives
up to expectations.**

Mixed grain jambalaya

8 skinless, boneless chicken thighs, halved

1 tbsp seasoned potato flour (see page 86)

1 tbsp vegetable oil

¼lb raw garlic sausage, roughly chopped and lightly dry-fried

¼lb chorizo sausage, roughly chopped and lightly dry-fried

1 onion, finely chopped

1 garlic clove, finely chopped

½ red pepper, cored, seeded, and cut into ½in dice

½ green pepper, cored, seeded, and cut into ½in dice

1 tsp soft thyme leaves

1 red chile, seeded and roughly chopped

8oz can chopped tomatoes

2 cups chicken stock

¼ cup pearl barley, soaked in water for 30 minutes and drained

½ cup brown basmati rice, rinsed

1 tbsp millet seeds, dry-fried until they "pop"

8 jumbo shrimp, shelled and deveined

3 tbsp pumpkin seeds

1 heaping cup thinly sliced okra

2 tbsp finely chopped flat-leaf parsley

salt and freshly ground black pepper

1. Dust the chicken in the potato flour. Put the oil in a large nonstick skillet over high heat, add the chicken, and the dry-fried garlic and chorizo sausages and lightly brown, then remove and set aside.

2. Add the onion, garlic, peppers, thyme, and chile to the same skillet and cook over medium heat for 8 minutes, stirring continuously, to soften the onion. Place in the slow cooker with the meat.

3. Add the tomatoes and chicken stock. Cover and cook on low for about 5–8 hours, until the chicken is almost cooked.

4. Remove the lid and add the pearl barley, rice, and millet, cover, and cook for 1½ hours, until the chicken is thoroughly cooked and the grains tender. Turn the slow cooker to high, fold in the jumbo shrimp, pumpkin seeds, and okra, cover, and cook for a further 40 minutes. Finally, fold in the parsley and season to taste.

To shell and devein shrimp
Start at the large end and peel away the shell. To devein, cut a shallow slit down the middle of the outside curve of each shrimp, using a sharp, pointed knife. Pull out the dark vein, then rinse the cut under cold running water.

SERVES
4

PREP
20 MINS

MARINATE
1 HR

COOKING
6½–8½
HRS

SETTING
LOW &
HIGH

This is an unusual chicken dish inspired by a lovely lady from Trinidad, who taught me that you never chop up a Scotch bonnet chile when cooking a stew, but always leave it whole so you can fish it out when the dish has reached the required chile heat.

Caribbean chicken stew

8 chicken thighs, skin on

juice of 1 lemon

1 tbsp salt

2 onions, roughly chopped

4 garlic cloves, roughly chopped

2 tsp soft thyme leaves

2 bay leaves

3 tbsp tomato ketchup

1 tbsp Worcestershire sauce

¾lb chicken livers, cleaned and halved

4 tbsp canola or vegetable oil

4 tbsp Demerara sugar

2 cups chicken stock, hot

1 Scotch bonnet chile, left whole

2 tbsp grated creamed coconut
  (from a solid block)

⅓ cup heavy cream

salt and freshly ground black pepper

to serve

steamed vegetables or rice

boiled potatoes

1. Place the chicken in a bowl. Mix with the lemon juice and salt. Leave for 5 minutes then rinse, drain, and pat dry with paper towels.

2. Place the onions, garlic, thyme, bay leaves, ketchup, and Worcestershire sauce in a blender and process to a smooth paste.

3. Spoon half the paste over the chicken and toss to combine. Then do the same to the chicken livers. Leave both to marinate for 1 hour.

4. Split the oil and sugar between 2 skillets over medium heat and stir until the sugar dissolves and begins to caramelize. Continue to heat until deep golden. Wipe the marinade from the chicken and the livers. Add the chicken to one pan and the livers to the other. Stir both to coat with the caramel and cook for 2 minutes.

5. Place the chicken with the marinade and sugars in your slow cooker, pour on the stock, add the chile, cover, and cook on low for 6–8 hours.

6. Increase the heat to high and add the chicken livers, grated coconut, and cream, then stir to combine. Cook for 30–40 minutes, check the seasoning, and remove the chile.

7. Serve with steamed vegetables or rice, and boiled potatoes.

SERVES
4–6

PREP
20 MINS

COOKING
7–8 HRS

SETTING
LOW

Simple country fare with a superb combination of flavors that everyone will love. Offer a glass of hard cider or a fruity white wine to go with it.

Sausages, chicken, apples, and plums

2 tbsp olive oil

1lb Toulouse or garlic sausages, cut into ½in slices

8 chicken thighs, skin on

4 tbsp sherry vinegar

1¼ cups chicken stock

⅔ cup dry white wine

2 bay leaves

4 sage leaves

2 thyme sprigs

16 plums or greengages, halved and stoned

8 garlic cloves, halved lengthways

2 large all-purpose apples, peeled, cored, and cut into 1in cubes

2 tbsp Dijon mustard

12 new potatoes, halved

2 tbsp unsalted butter, diced

1 tbsp finely chopped mint

3 tbsp finely chopped flat-leaf parsley

salt and freshly ground black pepper

to serve

crusty bread

buttered cabbage

1. Heat the oil in a skillet and brown the sausages and chicken in batches over high heat. Remove with a slotted spoon and set aside.

2. Pour off most of the oil from the skillet, add the vinegar, and bring to a boil, scraping anything that sticks to the bottom and stirring together. Add the stock, wine, bay leaves, sage, and thyme, then spoon into the slow cooker. Add the plums, garlic, apple, mustard, potatoes, sausages, and chicken and stir to combine. Cover and cook on low for 7–8 hours until the meat is cooked.

3. Add the butter, mint, and parsley, and swirl to combine. Taste and check the seasoning.

4. Serve with crusty bread and some buttered cabbage, if you like.

SERVES
4

PREP
20 MINS

COOKING
8 HRS

SETTING
LOW

Home-made baked beans by any other name. There are loads of flavors going into this dish, but they balance well by the end of the slow cooking. This is great as an accompaniment to grilled meat or fish, or just as a supper dish on its own with some toasted bread.

Chili beans with chorizo and tomato

2 tbsp olive oil

1lb chorizo sausage, skin removed and cut into bite-sized chunks

4oz pancetta, diced

2 red onions, finely chopped

1 celery stalk, finely chopped

1 large carrot, finely chopped

1 long mild red chile, finely chopped

½ tsp dried red pepper flakes

1 tsp smoked paprika

1 tsp dried oregano

2 tbsp tomato paste

2 x 14oz cans chopped tomatoes

14oz can peeled cherry tomatoes

1 tbsp dark muscovado sugar

¾ cup chicken stock, boiling or hot

2 x 14oz cans cannellini beans, drained and rinsed

salt and freshly ground black pepper

2 tbsp roughly chopped flat-leaf parsley

to serve

garlic-rubbed toasted ciabatta bread

1. Heat the oil in a large skillet and cook the chorizo chunks over medium heat for 5 minutes, stirring occasionally, to release the delicious paprika-flavored fat. Remove the chorizo with a slotted spoon, leaving the fat behind, and set aside.

2. Cook the pancetta, onions, celery, and carrot in the same pan over medium heat for 8 minutes, to soften rather than color. Add the chile, paprika, oregano, and tomato paste, stir to combine, then spoon into your slow cooker. Add the remaining ingredients, except the seasoning and parsley, cover, and cook on low for 8 hours.

3. Check the seasoning, then stir in the parsley. Serve with garlic-rubbed toasted ciabatta bread.

Also try

Instead of the chorizo, try using your favorite pork sausage. Just remove the skin, cut into chunks, and cook in the same way.

SERVES
4

PREP
30 MINS

COOKING
8–10 HRS

SETTING
LOW &
HIGH

Even if I say so myself, and others have said so too, I make a mean chili.
Instead of using cocoa powder, you could grate in 1oz dark chocolate
(more than 70% cocoa solids) just before serving. This idea has its roots
in a Mexican *mole* (sauce), which often includes chocolate.

Chunky pork and beef chili

¼ cup olive oil

1½lb stewing beef, cut into ½in cubes

1½lb shoulder of pork, cut
into 1cm (½in) cubes

1lb smoked bacon, diced

3lb onions, finely chopped

2 tbsp finely chopped garlic

3 celery stalks, finely diced

5 mild red chiles, finely chopped

2 tbsp dried oregano

1 tbsp fennel seeds

2 tbsp ground cumin

2 tbsp paprika

1 tbsp ground coriander

2 tsp freshly ground black pepper

2 tsp ground cinnamon

1 tsp cayenne (to taste)

up to 4 cups beef stock,
boiling or hot

2 x 14oz cans chopped tomatoes

2 bay leaves

1 tbsp cocoa powder (unsweetened)

3 tbsp tomato paste

2 x 14oz cans red kidney beans,
drained and rinsed

salt and freshly ground black pepper

4 tbsp roughly chopped cilantro leaves

1. Put the oil in a large skillet over high heat and brown the beef and pork all over, working in batches if necessary. Remove with a slotted spoon and place in your slow cooker.

2. In the same pan, cook the bacon, onions, garlic, celery, and chiles in the oil for 8–10 minutes, stirring occasionally, until the bacon is golden brown. Add the dried oregano, fennel seeds, and ground spices and cook for a further 2 minutes.

3. Add the bacon mix and half the stock to the slow cooker, then add the remaining ingredients, except the beans, seasoning, and cilantro, and stir to combine. Cover and cook for on low for 6–8 hours, stirring occasionally, until the meat is cooked and tender.

4. Add the beans, pouring in some extra stock as required to ensure the beans are submerged. Turn the slow cooker to high, cover, and cook for a further 2 hours, adding extra stock if necessary. Season to taste and fold in the cilantro.

SERVING SUGGESTION
Serve with long-grain rice and any of the following garnishes: tortilla (soft or chips), guacamole, tomato salsa, finely sliced red onion, lime wedges, sour cream and grated Monterey Jack cheese.

Reducing the sauce
If the sauce is too thin at the end of the cooking time, transfer all the mixture to a large pan and boil vigorously until it has been reduced to the desired consistency.

A bowl of this will nourish you in every way. It's a soup-cum-stew packed with flavor and very affordable. Vegetarians please feel free to remove the meat and substitute vegetable stock for the chicken. It's the barley that transports me straight back, across the years, to my grandmother and childhood.

Barley with greens, sausage, and ham

1 stick unsalted butter

2 onions, finely chopped

2 garlic cloves, finely chopped

½ tsp soft thyme leaves

2 handfuls mixed spring greens and arugula, roughly chopped

2 heaping cups pearl barley, rinsed and drained

2oz Parma or Serrano ham, finely chopped

½ tsp ground cayenne

4 cups chicken stock

2 handfuls baby spinach

½ cup grated Parmesan

4 tbsp chopped flat-leaf parsley

2 tbsp snipped chives

2 tbsp pine nuts, toasted

salt and freshly ground black pepper

4oz chorizo sausage, thinly sliced

1. Melt half the butter in a saucepan over medium heat. Add the onions, garlic, and thyme. Cook for 8 minutes, until the onions have started to soften but not color. Transfer to your slow cooker.

2. Stir in the chopped greens, then fold in the barley, Parma ham, cayenne, and chicken stock. Cover and cook on low for 4–6 hours.

3. Add the spinach, Parmesan, parsley, chives, and pine nuts, stir to combine, then cover and cook on high for 15 minutes. Season to taste.

4. Just before the end of the cooking time, melt the remaining butter in a skillet and cook the chorizo slices over high heat, turning once, until browned and crisp on both sides.

5. Spoon the stew into 4 warm bowls and top with slices of crisp chorizo and a drizzle of the chorizo fat.

Curries
&
tagines

Red vegetable curry

see page 164

A recipe that's not just for vegetarians. We should all be eating less meat and more vegetables, but if you're going to swap vegetables for meat, do put loads of flavoring into the dish.

Chickpea and vegetable curry

2 large onions, roughly chopped

1 tbsp grated fresh ginger

4 tbsp good olive oil

1 tbsp finely chopped garlic

1 cinnamon stick

1 tsp ground turmeric

1 tsp garam masala

2 red chiles, finely sliced

14oz can chopped tomatoes

2 crushed green cardamom pods

6 cloves

1 tsp black peppercorns

1 tsp toasted cumin seeds

½lb new potatoes, halved

½ cauliflower, broken into small florets

3 carrots, halved lengthways

14oz can chickpeas, drained and rinsed

1 tbsp finely chopped mint

2 tbsp roughly chopped cilantro leaves

½lb baby spinach, washed

salt and freshly ground black pepper

1. Blend half the onion and the ginger to a smooth paste in a mini food processor and set aside.

2. In a large skillet, cook the remaining onion in the olive oil with the garlic and cinnamon over medium heat for 8 minutes, until the onions have softened but not colored. Spoon the mixture into the slow cooker and add all the remaining ingredients except the fresh herbs and spinach. Cover and cook on low for 6–8 hours until the root vegetables are tender.

3. Turn the heat to high, fold in the mint, cilantro, and spinach and season to taste. Cover and cook for 1 hour. Serve immediately.

4. Serve with rice or as part of an Indian thali or buffet.

SERVES
4–6

PREP
25 MINS

COOKING
4–5 HRS

SETTING
LOW

Even the most ardent meat-eater should try to eat more vegetarian food to improve their diet. So why not make the effort to create a curried chickpea dish? This one is bursting with delicious flavors.

Ghugni

1 large bay leaf

5 green cardamom pods

3 cloves

1in cinnamon stick

1 tsp each cumin and coriander seeds

¼ cup vegetable oil

2 potatoes, cut into 1in dice

½ fresh coconut, flesh finely sliced

1 large onion, finely chopped

1 tsp chili powder

½ tsp fennel seeds, crushed

8oz can chopped tomatoes

2 tsp ground turmeric

2 x 14oz cans chickpeas, drained, and rinsed

2 cups vegetable stock

2 tbsp thick tamarind paste

1 tsp finely chopped garlic

2 tsp grated jaggery (palm sugar) or soft light brown sugar

pinch of salt

¼ tsp each ground cumin and chili powder

to garnish

1in piece of fresh ginger

2 medium green chiles, sliced

2 tbsp roughly chopped cilantro

to serve

basmati rice

green salad

1. Dry-roast the bay leaf, cardamoms, cloves, cinnamon, and the cumin and coriander seeds in a skillet for 1–2 minutes, then grind to a fine powder in a mortar and pestle or electric coffee grinder.

2. Heat the oil in skillet, then fry the diced potato over medium heat until light golden brown. Add the coconut and onion to the skillet and fry until just turning light brown. Spoon into your slow cooker.

3. Add the chili powder, spice mix, fennel seeds, tomatoes, turmeric, chickpeas, and stock. Stir to combine, cover, and cook on low for 4–5 hours.

4. Near the end of the cooking time, mix the tamarind with 1 tbsp hot water, the garlic, jaggery, salt, cumin, and chili powder. When the jaggery has dissolved, drizzle this on top of the curried chickpeas.

5. For the garnish, slice the fresh ginger into very thin strips and then fry until crisp. Scatter over the ghugni with the sliced green chiles and the chopped cilantro.

6. Serve with basmati rice and an herby green salad.

SERVES
4

PREP
15 MINS

COOKING
3¾–4¾ HRS

SETTING
LOW

This is a lentil dish to die for. I even love it at room temperature as part of a buffet. It's not at all difficult to make, and the spices turn the lentils a golden color.

Spiced vegetable dhal with coconut flavors

2 tbsp vegetable oil

2 medium onions, grated

4 garlic cloves, crushed to a paste with a little sea salt

1 carrot, finely diced

1 celery stalk, finely diced

2 tsp ground cumin

1 tsp ground coriander

½ tsp ground fennel

2 tsp black or yellow mustard seeds

2 tsp ground turmeric

1 tsp chili powder

1 tsp grated fresh ginger

½lb split red lentils, rinsed and drained

1¼ cups vegetable stock, boiling

8oz can chopped tomatoes

1¾ cups coconut milk

1 bunch cilantro, roughly chopped

juice and grated zest of 1 unwaxed or organic lemon

1 tsp garam masala

1 cup green beans, topped, tailed and cut into ½in pieces

¼ cup coconut flakes or desiccated coconut

1. Heat the oil in a skillet, then cook the onions, garlic, carrot, and celery over medium heat for 6–8 minutes, stirring occasionally, until the vegetables are starting to soften but not color.

2. Add the spices and ginger and cook for 2 minutes. Transfer the mixture to your slow cooker, then add the lentils, stock, tomatoes, and coconut milk, and stir to combine. Cover and cook on low for 3–4 hours, stirring once.

3. Remove the lid and fold in the cilantro, lemon juice and zest, garam masala, and green beans. Cook, uncovered, for 40 minutes. Sprinkle with coconut flakes, which you could toast if you wish.

SERVES
4

PREP
25 MINS

COOKING
6¼–8¼
HRS

SETTING
LOW &
HIGH

Are artichokes worth the hassle? Only you can be the judge of that. I love them and with all the flavors going on here you've got yourself one heck of a vegetarian dish. So, if you're unsure, try them.

Stewed artichoke tagine

juice of 1 lemon

4 large globe artichokes

2 garlic cloves, roughly chopped

10 black peppercorns, crushed

12 coriander seeds, toasted and crushed

¼ tsp ground turmeric

pinch of ground cayenne

¼ tsp toasted cumin seeds

2 onions, cut vertically into eighths

2 bay leaves

¼ cup extra-virgin olive oil

pinch of saffron strands, soaked in
    2 tbsp cold water

2 carrots, thinly sliced

1¼ cups vegetable stock

8 dried apricots, thinly sliced

½ cup raisins

¼ cup flaked almonds

14oz can chickpeas, drained and rinsed

½lb baby spinach

2 tbsp roughly chopped cilantro

4 tbsp roughly chopped flat-leaf parsley

salt and freshly ground black pepper

to serve

couscous or long-grain rice

1. Fill a large bowl with cold water and add the lemon juice. Trim each artichoke by peeling the stem until all the woody matter has disappeared. Pull off the tough outer leaves until you reach the pale green ones. Cut about 1in off the top of each artichoke. Cut the artichokes vertically into 4, then cut or pull out the choke (the hairy part in the middle) and discard. Rub all the cut surfaces with the squeezed lemon pieces and place the prepared artichokes in the bowl of water.

2. In a mortar and pestle or an electric coffee grinder crush the garlic, peppercorns, coriander seeds, turmeric, cayenne, and cumin to a powder.

3. Cook the onions and bay leaves in a skillet with the olive oil, over medium heat, for about 8 minutes, until soft but not colored. Add the spice mix and cook for a further 3 minutes. Stir to combine.

4. Add the artichokes and the saffron with its soaking liquor, and toss to combine. Add the carrots, half the vegetable stock, apricots, raisins, and almonds, and stir to combine. Cover and cook on low for about 6–8 hours.

5. When the artichokes are tender, add the chickpeas, spinach, cilantro, and parsley, and stir to combine. Turn to high, cover and cook for 15 minutes.

6. Season to taste. Serve hot or cold with steamed couscous or rice.

SERVES
4

PREP
40 MINS

COOKING
4¼–6¼ HRS

SETTING
LOW & HIGH

This recipe has its roots in Thailand, where red curry is a national favorite. It's cheap to make and very filling and nutritious.

13½fl oz can coconut milk

½ cup vegetable stock

2 carrots, diced

1 large onion, roughly chopped

8 garlic cloves, sliced

1 red pepper, cored, seeded, and roughly diced

1 scant cup sweet potato, cut into 1in chunks

½ pumpkin or butternut squash, peeled, seeded, and cut into 1in chunks

1 cup green beans, trimmed

2 zucchini, cut into 1in disks

¾ cup frozen petits pois, defrosted

1 bunch scallions, finely chopped

3 tbsp roughly chopped cilantro

1 tbsp lime juice

1 tbsp Thai fish sauce (nam pla)

salt and freshly ground black pepper

for the curry paste

10 black peppercorns

2 tsp each cumin and coriander seeds

10 mild red chiles, seeded

5 shallots, finely chopped

2 garlic cloves, crushed

¾in piece of fresh ginger, chopped

6 lemongrass stalks, tough outer leaves removed, roughly chopped

grated zest of 1 lime

pinch of ground cinnamon

½ tsp ground turmeric

1 tbsp superfine sugar

½ tsp salt

splash each of vegetable and chile oil

Red vegetable curry

1. To make the curry paste: fry the peppercorns and the cumin and coriander seeds until fragrant in a dry skillet over medium heat, then grind them to a powder in a mortar and pestle or electric coffee grinder.

2. Put this powder and all the other curry paste ingredients, except the oils, into a food processor and blend until smooth (it takes a good 5–10 minutes), adding a splash of water as necessary to help the process.

3. Warm the oils in a skillet and add 2½ tbsp of paste. Cook on low heat until it becomes fragrant, stir to combine, then add to your slow cooker with the coconut milk, stock, carrots, onion, garlic, red pepper, sweet potato, and pumpkin. Cover and cook on low for 4–6 hours.

4. Add the green beans, zucchini, peas, and scallions. Cook, uncovered, on high for 15 minutes. Fold in the cilantro, lime juice, and Thai fish sauce, and season to taste.

5. Garnish with sliced green chiles, lime wedges or halves, and cilantro leaves, and serve with steamed basmati rice.

SERVES
4–5

PREP
20 MINS

COOKING
7–9 HRS

SETTING
LOW & HIGH

If I were vegetarian, I would get the majority of my diet from the Indian subcontinent and the Far East, where delicious things are done to vegetables, so much so, that meat and fish could become a distant memory. Despite the length of the ingredient list, this is a very straightforward recipe.

Kashmiri spiced vegetables

2 tsp cumin seeds, toasted

1 tsp coriander seeds, toasted

1 tsp fennel seeds

seeds from 2 green cardamom pods and 1 black cardamom pod (optional)

½ tsp ground cinnamon

3 garlic cloves, crushed to a paste with a little sea salt

½ tsp ground black pepper

½ tsp salt

1 tsp grated fresh ginger

1 tsp chili powder

½ tsp ground turmeric

2 tbsp vegetable oil

1 onion, roughly chopped

2 large potatoes, cubed

1 sweet potato, cubed

1 small cauliflower, broken into florets

¾ cup canned chopped tomatoes

1¼ cups vegetable stock

⅔ cup plain, strained yogurt

1¼ cups frozen peas, defrosted

2 handfuls baby spinach

1 tbsp cilantro leaves

2 mild green chiles, seeded, and thinly sliced

2 ripe tomatoes, each cut into 6 wedges

¼ cup toasted flaked almonds

to serve

basmati rice

1. Put the cumin seeds, coriander seeds, fennel seeds, and cardamom seeds into an electric coffee grinder, or mortar and pestle, and grind to a fine powder. Then mix with the cinnamon, garlic, black pepper, salt, ginger, chili powder, and turmeric.

2. Meanwhile, heat the oil in a skillet and cook the onion over medium heat for about 6–8 minutes until soft but without much color. Then add the spice paste, mix well, and cook for a further 2 minutes. Transfer to your slow cooker with the potatoes, cauliflower, tomatoes, stock, and yogurt, then stir to combine. Cover and cook on low for 6–8 hours.

3. Increase the setting to high, remove the lid, then fold in the peas, spinach, cilantro leaves, green chiles, and fresh tomatoes, then cook, uncovered, for 1 hour.

4. Scatter the almonds over the top and serve with basmati rice.

SERVES 4 · PREP 25 MINS · COOKING 3½ HRS · SETTING LOW & HIGH

Salmon can be a bit bland and needs a little something to pep it up. But then again, salmon is a perfect fish for taking on powerful flavors.

2 tbsp canola or vegetable oil

1 onion, finely chopped

2 lemongrass stalks, tough outer leaves removed, roughly chopped

2 fresh kaffir lime leaves, central stalks removed

3 garlic cloves, roughly chopped

1½in piece of fresh ginger, finely sliced

1 tsp ground coriander

3 tbsp finely chopped cilantro stalks and leaves

1 tsp chili powder

1 tsp ground turmeric

1 cup coconut milk

7oz can pineapple pulp in juice, drained

4 x 6oz skinless salmon fillets

1 tbsp Thai fish sauce (nam pla)

2 tbsp lime juice

salt and freshly ground black pepper

to garnish

2 scallions, finely sliced

2 green chiles, seeded and finely sliced

1 tbsp coriander leaves

to serve

basmati rice

Salmon in a spiced coconut cream

1. Place 1 tbsp oil in a food processor with the onion, lemongrass, lime leaves, garlic, ginger, ground coriander, chopped cilantro, chili powder, and turmeric. Blend until fairly smooth.

2. In a skillet, heat the remaining oil and gently cook the spice paste for 2–3 minutes, not allowing it to color too much. Spoon this mixture into your slow cooker, then add the coconut milk and pineapple pulp. Cover and cook on low for 2 hours.

3. Add the salmon, replace the lid, and continue to cook on low for 1 hour, then increase the setting to high and cook, uncovered, for 30 minutes. Remove the salmon steaks to a warm dish, cover loosely with foil, and keep warm.

4. Fold the Thai fish sauce and lime juice into the spiced coconut sauce and season to taste. Spoon over the salmon, then scatter with the scallions, sliced chiles, and cilantro leaves. Serve with rice.

Pineapple pulp
If you can't find pineapple pulp, just blend some canned or fresh pineapple to a pulp instead.

SERVES
4–6

PREP
30 MINS

MARINATE
20 MINS

COOKING
1½ HRS

SETTING
LOW

Goan fish curry

3 tbsp coconut milk

2oz tamarind paste, mixed with
2 tbsp water

1 tbsp runny honey

½ tsp salt

2¼lb pollock fillets (left whole),
skin on

1 tbsp Thai fish sauce (nam pla)

for the curry paste

1¼ cups desiccated coconut

10–12 black peppercorns

2 tsp dried red pepper flakes

1 tbsp ground coriander

10–12 garlic cloves, peeled

1 tbsp sesame seeds

1¼in piece of fresh ginger,
roughly chopped

for the tempering

3 tbsp vegetable oil

2 tbsp black mustard seeds

8–10 curry leaves

3 green chiles, slit lengthways,
seeded, and thinly sliced

to serve

basmati rice

1. Combine the coconut milk with the tamarind and water paste, half the honey, and the salt, then add the fish, cover, and marinate for 20 minutes. Drain and set aside, retaining the marinade.

2. In a food processor, blend together all the ingredients for the curry paste until smooth, adding a little marinade to facilitate the blending. Add the remaining marinade. Pour the mixture into your slow cooker and add the remaining honey, the Thai fish sauce, and the fish pieces. Cover and cook on low for 1½ hours.

3. Heat the oil in a skillet and add the mustard seeds, curry leaves, and green chiles. Cook on high heat, stirring continuously to prevent burning. When the chiles are flecked with brown, add the mixture to the curry.

4. Serve with rice.

Antony's tip
In Goa they use pomfret, but it's hard to find anywhere else, so do use any other firm-fleshed white fish such as cod or monkfish. Ask them to fillet the fish for you at the fish counter.

SERVES
4

PREP
20 MINS

COOKING
2¾ HRS

SETTING
LOW &
HIGH

The influence of curry does wonders for good white fish and slow cooking works well, too. If you want to add a selection of green vegetables to bulk up the curry, add them at the same time as the fish.

A pleasant little fish curry

2 tbsp canola or vegetable oil

1 onion, finely chopped

1 garlic clove, crushed to a paste with
   a little sea salt

1 tsp grated fresh ginger

1 tsp ground cardamom

1 tsp ground coriander

½ tsp ground cumin

½ tsp ground fennel

1 tsp chili powder

1 tsp ground turmeric

½ tsp English mustard powder

1¼ cups coconut milk

8oz can chopped tomatoes

1½lb skinless firm white fish
   cut into 1in dice

salt and freshly ground black pepper

to garnish
tomato, seeded and diced
cilantro leaves

to serve
basmati rice

1. Heat the oil in a heavy-based pan or skillet over moderate heat. Add the onion, garlic, and ginger and cook for 8 minutes, until the onion is soft but not colored.

2. Meanwhile, mix the spices with 2 tbsp water to create a smooth paste, then fold into the softened onion and cook gently for a further 2 minutes, stirring regularly.

3. Transfer this mixture to your slow cooker, pour in the coconut milk and tomatoes, give it a little stir, cover, and cook on low for 2 hours.

4. Fold in the fish and cook, uncovered, on high for 45 minutes, until the fish is cooked through.

5. Season to taste, garnish with the diced tomato and cilantro leaves, and serve with rice.

SERVES
4

PREP
15 MINS

COOKING
2½–3½
HRS

SETTING
LOW &
HIGH

I'm a massive fan of kedgeree, a colonial dish from Britain's days in India where it was usually served at breakfast dish. I've made it healthier by adding mackerel, which is a good oily fish.

Smoked fish kedgeree

9oz skinless undyed smoked haddock cut into ¾in pieces

1 onion, finely sliced

1 leek, finely shredded

3 tbsp unsalted butter

2 tsp mild curry paste

1 tsp ground turmeric

2 bay leaves

1 cup easy-cook basmati rice, rinsed and drained

2 sachets dashi powder or 1 fish stock cube, crushed

3 tbsp heavy cream

1 smoked mackerel fillet, skinned and flaked

1 hot-smoked salmon fillet, flaked

3 hard-boiled eggs, roughly chopped

1 tbsp snipped chives

2 plum tomatoes, seeded and cut into small dice

1 tbsp finely chopped flat-leaf parsley

to serve

leafy salad

1. Pour boiling water over the smoked haddock and allow to sit for 10 minutes. Drain.

2. Meanwhile, in a skillet, cook the onion and leek gently in the butter for 6–8 minutes, until the onion has softened but not colored. Fold in the curry paste, turmeric, and bay leaves, stir to combine, then fold in the rice and stir to coat.

3. Transfer the rice mixture to your slow cooker and add 2½ cups boiling water with the dashi powder or stock cube. Stir to combine, then cover and cook on low for 2–3 hours, until the rice is tender and the liquid has been absorbed.

4. Fold in the haddock and the remaining ingredients, cover, and cook on high for 20 minutes. Serve with a well-dressed leafy salad.

SERVES
4

PREP
15 MINS

COOKING
4½ HRS

SETTING
LOW &
HIGH

Monkfish is the perfect fish for the slow cooker—it's meaty, has no bones, and stays intact. It may be expensive, but see this as a dish for entertaining that's well worth the expense.

Poached monkfish in spicy tomato sauce

1 tbsp canola or vegetable oil

1 onion, grated

4 garlic cloves, crushed to a paste with a little sea salt

2 red chiles, seeded and finely sliced

½ tsp chili powder

½ tsp ground turmeric

½ tsp ground cumin

½ tsp ground coriander

½ tsp ground fennel

2 green cardamom pods, crushed

⅔ cup passata

¼ cup fish or chicken stock

14oz can cannellini beans, drained and rinsed

juice of 2 limes

1½lb monkfish fillet, cut into 4 steaks

1¼ cups frozen peas, defrosted

1 tsp garam masala

1 tsp finely chopped mint

3 tbsp roughly chopped cilantro

salt and freshly ground black pepper

to serve

plain, strained yogurt

basmati rice

1. Heat the oil in a skillet and gently cook the onion, garlic, and chiles for 8 minutes, until the onion is soft but not colored. Add all the spices, except the garam masala, and cook for 1 minute, stirring to combine.

2. Transfer the onion mixture to your slow cooker. Stir in the passata, stock, cannellini beans, and lime juice. Cover and cook on low for 2½ hours.

3. Add the fish to the slow cooker with the peas. Increase the heat to high, cover, and cook for 1½ hours.

4. Lift the fish carefully from the sauce to a warmed dish and cover loosely with foil to keep warm.

5. Fold the garam masala and herbs into the sauce and cook, uncovered, for 20 minutes.

6. Season to taste, then spoon the spicy sauce over the fish. Top each portion with a dollop of yogurt and serve with rice.

SERVES
4–6

PREP
20 MINS

MARINATE
4 HRS

COOKING
6–7 HRS

SETTING
LOW

There are so many recipes for chicken wings, but I reckon this is my favorite. Give it a try and see what you think.

Sweet and spicy chicken wings

1 tbsp Szechwan peppercorns, toasted and ground

1 tbsp grated garlic

3 tbsp grated fresh ginger

4 tbsp grated orange zest,

4 scallions, cut into 1in pieces

1 red chile, finely chopped

2 tbsp runny honey

2 tbsp soy sauce

⅔ cup corn oil

2 tbsp sesame oil

2¼lb chicken wings, cut in half through the joint, tips discarded

salt and freshly ground black pepper

2 cups peach nectar

to garnish

2 tbsp finely chopped parsley

2 tbsp snipped chives

1. In a mini blender or mortar and pestle, blend the peppercorns, garlic, ginger, 3 tbsp orange zest, scallions, and chile until you have a rough paste.

2. In a large bowl, combine the honey, soy sauce, and oils with the paste and toss with the chicken wings. Season to taste. Cover with plastic wrap and leave to marinate for at least 4 hours, or preferably overnight, in the fridge.

3. Remove the chicken from the marinade and cook in a skillet over high heat, turning once, until the chicken is golden brown, then place in your slow cooker with the marinade and peach nectar. Cover and cook on low for 6–7 hours until the meat is cooked through.

4. Garnish with a mixture of the remaining orange zest, the chopped parsley and chives, and serve on its own as a snack or with rice.

Also try
You can also use drumsticks instead of chicken wings. The cooking time is exactly the same.

Zesting oranges
1 orange should produce 1 tbsp grated zest. Use organic oranges if available.

SERVES
4

PREP
30 MINS

MARINATE
30 MINS

COOKING
5½–6½
HRS

SETTING
LOW &
HIGH

Buttered chicken is a classic mild curry. It has loads of ingredients, but don't be discouraged. All are widely available so it's well worth making. You'll see I've used chicken thighs because I feel they give a sweet result, but if breasts are your thing, go for it.

2¼lb skinless boneless chicken thighs, halved

2 tbsp lemon juice

½ tsp salt

1 tsp chili powder

1¼ cups plain, strained yogurt

2 tsp ground ginger

2 tsp garam masala

1 stick unsalted butter

1 tbsp vegetable oil

2 onions, finely chopped

4 garlic cloves, crushed to a paste

1 tsp ground coriander

½ tsp each ground cumin and fennel

1 tsp sweet paprika

1⅔ cups passata

2 tbsp tomato paste

⅔ cup chicken stock

2 tbsp grated jaggery (palm sugar)

1 cinnamon stick, broken in half

3 tomatoes, roughly chopped

⅓ cup heavy cream

salt and freshly ground black pepper

to garnish
cilantro leaves
flaked almonds
scallions, sliced
3oz feta or paneer cheese

to serve
basmati or pilau rice

Buttered chicken and tomato curry

1. Place the chicken in a nonmetallic bowl and toss with the lemon juice, salt, and chili powder. Cover and marinate, ideally for 3–4 hours in the fridge, but for at least 30 minutes.

2. Whisk together the yogurt, ginger, and half the garam masala, pour over the marinated chicken, and mix well. Spoon the chicken mixture into the slow cooker.

3. Heat one-third of the butter with the oil in a skillet over low heat, then cook the onion with the garlic and spices for 8 minutes, until the onion has softened but has not much color. Stir the onion mixture into the chicken, then stir in the tomato passata, tomato paste, stock, jaggery, and cinnamon. Fold into the chicken mixture, cover with the lid, and cook on low for 5–6 hours, until the chicken is cooked through.

4. Fold in the remaining garam masala, fresh tomatoes, and cream, then cover and cook on high for 20 minutes.

5. Remove the chicken to a warm serving dish, then whisk the remaining butter into the sauce, making sure it is well emulsified. Check the seasoning, then pour the sauce over the chicken and garnish with cilantro leaves, almonds, and scallions. Just before serving, finley crumble the cheese and scatter it over the surface. Serve with basmati or pilau rice.

Palm sugar
If you can't find jaggery or palm sugar, use soft light brown sugar.

SERVES
4

PREP
30 MINS

COOKING
7½–8½
HRS

SETTING
LOW &
HIGH

Don't panic about the number of ingredients—if you're into curries you should have all the spices you'll need for this in your cupboard. What you have here is a genuine curry with two lentils, one of which stays intact while the other should start to break down.

Chicken, Puy lentil, and butternut curry

2 tbsp canola or vegetable oil

2 onions, finely chopped

3 garlic cloves, crushed to a paste with a little sea salt

2 tsp grated fresh ginger

1 tsp ground cumin

1 tsp ground fennel

1½ tsp ground coriander

1 tsp black mustard seeds

1 tsp chili powder

1 tsp ground turmeric

2 pints good chicken stock

2lb skinless, boneless chicken thighs, halved

14oz can chopped tomatoes

1 medium butternut squash, peeled, seeded and cut into bite-sized pieces

1⅔ cups coconut milk

¾ cup Puy lentils, rinsed and drained

¾ cup red lentils, rinsed and drained

2 tomatoes, cut into rough chunks

1¼ cups frozen peas, defrosted

salt and freshly ground black pepper

to garnish

red chiles, finely sliced

cilantro, roughly chopped

mint, finely chopped

to serve

basmati rice

1. Heat the oil in a large skillet over medium heat and cook the onion, garlic, and ginger for 8 minutes, until the onion has softened but has not much color. Add all the spices and cook for a further 5 minutes.

2. Add the stock and bring to a boil, then pour the mix into the slow cooker and add the chicken, canned tomatoes, butternut squash, half the coconut milk, and lentils. Stir to combine. Cover with the lid and cook on low for 7–8 hours until the chicken is cooked through.

3. Add the remaining coconut milk, fresh tomatoes, and peas, stir to combine, and cook, uncovered, on high for 25 minutes. Season to taste and garnish with the chiles, cilantro, and mint. Serve with rice.

SERVES
4

PREP
20 MINS

COOKING
8¼ HRS

SETTING
LOW &
HIGH

I was taught this dish in the Oriental Thai Cooking School in Bangkok,
which was a superb opportunity even if a little painful for the bank
balance. You could use a whole duck and get your butcher to cut it into
portions, but I use duck legs because they are so much cheaper.
This works very well with chicken and pork too.

Braised duck in red curry

6 duck legs, cut into 1in pieces
  (bone in) by a butcher

2 tbsp duck fat or vegetable oil

12 shallots, thinly sliced

6 garlic cloves, finely chopped

2 tbsp grated fresh ginger

2¾oz Thai red curry paste

13½fl oz can coconut milk

1 tbsp soft light brown sugar

3 fresh kaffir lime leaves, thinly sliced

2 tbsp lime juice

20 basil leaves, ripped

3 handfuls spinach

1 tbsp Thai fish sauce (nam pla)

to garnish

1 bunch cilantro, leaves only

1 bunch scallions, thinly sliced

2 green chiles, seeded and
  thinly sliced

to serve

Thai fragrant rice

1. Brown the duck pieces in a skillet with the duck fat over high heat.
Remove and set aside. Add the shallots and garlic to the pan and cook over
medium heat for about 8–10 minutes, until the shallots start to brown,
stirring from time to time.

2. Add the ginger and curry paste and cook for 3 minutes, stirring
continuously. Put the duck in your slow cooker and add the contents of the
skillet, coconut milk, sugar, and lime leaves. Cover and cook on low for
8 hours, until the duck is cooked through and tender.

3. Add the lime juice, basil leaves, spinach, and Thai fish sauce, stir to
combine, then cook, uncovered, on high for 15 minutes.

4. Garnish with the cilantro leaves, scallions, and chiles, and serve with Thai
fragrant rice.

SERVES
4

PREP
20 MINS

COOKING
8–10 HRS

SETTING
LOW

My friend Merrilees Parker introduced me to a version of this curry after her travels in India. I've changed it a fair bit to reflect my taste, but it's a delicious change from kleftiko or braised lamb shanks with rosemary and garlic.

Kerala curried lamb shanks

⅓ cup canola or vegetable oil

6 green cardamom pods, lightly crushed

1 cinnamon stick, broken in half

2 star anise, broken into small pieces

1 tsp cumin seeds

½ tsp coriander seeds

½ tsp fennel seeds

2 onions, finely chopped

2in piece of fresh ginger,
  roughly chopped

6 large medium-hot green chiles,
  roughly chopped

½ tsp chili powder

2 tsp ground turmeric

2 x 14oz cans chopped tomatoes

1 tbsp tomato paste

1 tbsp grated jaggery (palm sugar)
  or soft light brown sugar

1 cup chicken stock

1 cup coconut cream

4 lamb shanks, soaked in cold water
  for 30 minutes and drained

to serve
basmati rice

1. Heat the oil in a skillet. Add the cardamom, cinnamon, and star anise, and the cumin, coriander, and fennel seeds. Cook for 2 minutes over low heat until fragrant. Remove and set aside, leaving the oil in the skillet.

2. Meanwhile, in a food processor, blend together the onions, ginger, chiles, chili powder, and turmeric to make a smooth paste. Spoon this paste into the spiced oil and fry gently for 8 minutes, until lightly browned. Put this mixture and the cooked spices, tomatoes, tomato paste, jaggery, stock, and coconut cream into your slow cooker.

3. Place the lamb shanks in the curry sauce. Cover and cook on low for 8–10 hours until the meat is cooked and almost falling off the bone. Remove the shanks gently to a serving dish, then skim off the majority of the fat from the surface of the sauce.

4. Pour the sauce over the shanks and serve with basmati rice.

SERVES 4

PREP 30 MINS

COOKING 2½–3 HRS

STOVE

Slow cooking doesn't just mean European flavors, as this superb "dry" curry from Malaysia illustrates. If making in a slow cooker, the sauce will be wetter because there will not be the same evaporation, but it will be none the less delicious.

for the rendang paste

2 onions, roughly chopped

1½in piece of fresh ginger, chopped

1 tbsp roughly chopped galangal (or another tsp roughly chopped ginger)

4 garlic cloves

2 lemongrass stalks, tough outer leaves removed, roughly chopped

2 tsp ground turmeric

6 long, dried red chiles, soaked in water for 30 minutes and drained

2 tbsp vegetable oil

6 green cardamom pods, crushed

1 cinnamon stick, broken in half

1½lb braising or stewing steak, cut into 2in cubes

13½fl oz can coconut milk

6 kaffir lime leaves, fresh or dried

grated zest of 2 organic limes

1¼ cups beef stock

⅔ cup desiccated coconut

2 tbsp tamarind paste or juice of 2 limes

2 tbsp finely chopped cilantro

to garnish

cilantro sprigs

lime cheeks (slice either side of core)

to serve

basmati rice

Beef rendang

1. First make the rendang paste: place all the ingredients in a food processor and blend to a smooth paste.

2. Heat a skillet and add the oil. Fry the paste over high heat for about 3 minutes until it darkens and is aromatic. Add the crushed cardamom pods and cinnamon and cook for another minute.

3. Add the beef and fry it in the paste, stirring all the time, until it is well sealed.

4. Pour over the coconut milk and bring to a gentle simmer. Add the kaffir lime leaves and lime zest. Season with salt and stir well. Cook very gently for 2½–3 hours, uncovered, stirring frequently. Add more stock if the sauce gets too dry. The meat should be really tender and cooked through, and the sauce greatly reduced and almost dry.

5. Meanwhile, toast the coconut in a dry skillet, watching it carefully because it burns easily. Blitz to a powder in a small blender or electric coffee grinder, or use a mortar and pestle. When the rendang is ready, stir the coconut into the curry with the tamarind paste or lime juice and the chopped cilantro.

6. Garnish with a few sprigs of cilantro and lime cheeks and serve immediately with basmati rice.

To make this in a slow cooker
Reduce the amount of stock by half. In step 4 cover and cook for 6–8 hours on low, then turn the slow cooker to high and cook for 1½ hours. Add more hot stock if the sauce gets too dry.

Desserts
&
treats

Baked chocolate custard cups

see page 192

A chocolate saucy pudding **188**

Chocolate-baked cheesecake with a brownie twist **190**

Baked chocolate custard cups **192**

Rich maple crème caramel **194**

Marmalade-brioche baked custard **196**

Treacle sponge **197**

Baked Lebanese fruit with melting blue cheese **198**

Spiced apple terrine and honeyed yogurt **200**

Baked fruit and nut apples **202**

Poached quince with vanilla yogurt mousse **204**

Jamaican coconut bananas **205**

Poached figs with blackberries **206**

Compote of pears, prunes, oranges, and walnuts in spiced wine **208**

Braised pear with Roquefort **210**

Spiced carrot cake with cream-cheese frosting **212**

A Christmas quantity of classic mincemeat **214**

A pleasant lemon curd **215**

SERVES 4

PREP
15 MINS

COOKING
2½–3
HRS

SETTING
HIGH

A classic that has stood the test of time and that I'm sure has been produced in many households. It's a must with your slow cooker!

A chocolate saucy pudding

6½ tbsp unsalted butter,
  plus extra for greasing
¾ cup milk
1 tsp vanilla extract
1¼ cup superfine sugar
1 egg, beaten
2 cups self-rising flour
½ tsp baking powder
4 tbsp good cocoa powder
1¼ cups soft light brown sugar
2½ cups boiling water

1. Lightly grease your slow cooker bowl.

2. Melt the butter in the milk over low heat. Remove from the heat and whisk in the vanilla extract and superfine sugar, until the sugar has dissolved. Stir in the egg.

3. Sift together the flour, baking powder, and 2 tbsp cocoa powder, and fold into the milk mixture.

4. Spoon the mixture over the bottom of the cooker bowl and level the surface, then evenly sift the brown sugar and the remaining cocoa powder over the top. Gently pour the boiling water over the sugared batter, cover, and cook on high for 2½–3 hours until the center is firm. Remove the bowl from the cooker and allow to stand for 10 minutes before serving.

SERVING SUGGESTION
This is good with whipped cream or ice cream or both, but beware, it's not to be eaten on a regular basis!

MAKES
9

PREP
30 MINS +
REFRIGERATE
1 HR

COOKING
2¼ HRS

SETTING
HIGH

The brownie is one of our best-sellers at both The Greyhound pub in Oxfordshire and our deli, Windsor Larder. Adding the cheesecake topping creates a great combination of two hugely popular desserts.

Chocolate-baked cheesecake with a brownie twist

3oz semisweet dark chocolate (70% cocoa solids), roughly chopped

6½ tbsp unsalted butter, roughly diced

2½ tsp superfine sugar

2 eggs, beaten

⅓ cup all-purpose flour

½ tsp baking powder

1½oz milk chocolate, cut into small chunks

1½oz white chocolate, cut into small chunks

½ cup pecans (optional)

2 tbsp mini marshmallows

for the cheesecake topping

¾ cup full-fat cream cheese

3½ tbsp superfine sugar

1 tsp vanilla extract

1 egg, beaten

to serve

vanilla ice cream

1. Line the base and sides of a 6in square cake pan with nonstick parchment paper.

2. Pour 2¾in hot water into the ceramic slow cooker bowl and turn to high. Put an upturned saucer or plate in the bottom of the slow cooker. Place the dark chocolate and butter in a heatproof bowl, put in the slow cooker, and leave for about 10 minutes until the chocolate has melted. Remove the bowl from the slow cooker.

3. Meanwhile, make the cheesecake topping by beating together the cream cheese, superfine sugar, and vanilla extract. Then gradually whisk the egg into the mixture until it's very smooth.

4. Stir the chocolate and butter together until smooth and velvety, then whisk in the sugar. Gradually beat in the egg until combined (it may look as if it's splitting, but have no fear). Sift the flour and baking powder over the mixture and carefully fold them in with the chocolate chunks and nuts, if using. Spoon the mixture into your cake pan, level the surface, and dot with the mini marshmallows.

5. Place small dollops of cheesecake topping onto the surface of the chocolate mixture and then, using a fork, swirl the cheesecake and brownie mixtures together to get a marbled effect.

6. Cover the cake pan with foil, then place on the upturned saucer in the bottom of the slow cooker. Pour more boiling water into the slow cooker to just over halfway up the sides of the cake pan, cover, and cook on high for 2¼ hours, until almost set in the center. Cool the cake in the pan on a rack.

7. Turn out and refrigerate for at least 1 hour, then cut into 9 squares. Serve with vanilla ice cream.

SERVES
6

PREP
20 MINS

5 QUART
COOKING
2 HRS
LARGE POT

SETTING
HIGH

**What could be nicer than baked custard with chocolate magic—
a classic French concept. It's equally good served hot or cold as
a mousse, and it can be made well in advance.**

Baked chocolate
custard cups

2 cups heavy cream

1 cup full-fat milk

1 vanilla pod, split lengthways and
    seeds scraped out

2 tbsp good cocoa powder

6oz semisweet dark chocolate
    (more than 55% cocoa solids),
    finely chopped

2 eggs

4 egg yolks

⅔ cup superfine sugar

to serve
cream
good cocoa powder, for dusting

1. Place the cream, milk, vanilla pod and seeds, cocoa powder, and
semisweet dark chocolate in a saucepan over medium heat and bring to
a boil to melt the chocolate, stirring from time to time. Remove from the
heat and set aside.

2. Place the eggs and yolks with the sugar in a bowl and whisk until pale and
ribboning. Gradually add the chocolate cream and whisk well to combine.
Strain the chocolate custard into 6 teacups or ramekins, place in the slow
cooker, and carefully pour boiling water around them to come halfway up
the sides. Cover and cook on high for 2 hours, until set.

3. Remove from the water bath and allow to cool for 5 minutes before
serving. Dust with cocoa powder and serve with cream.

Also try
If youare making this as a dessert for adults, add a couple of shots of liqueur—Kahlúa, coffee, or
chocolate—when heating the cream mixture.

SERVES 6 | 30 PREP MINS + REFRIGERATE 5 HRS | COOKING 3–3½ HRS | SETTING LOW

I learned this recipe in California. It's a cross between crème caramel and crème brûlée but without its sugar topping. The maple syrup gives it a delicious flavor, enhanced by the lovely runny caramel.

Rich maple crème caramel

1½ cups superfine sugar

2 cup heavy cream

½ cup full-fat milk

½ cup pure maple syrup

2 eggs

6 egg yolks

1. Make a caramel by gently dissolving the sugar in 1 cup water in a small heavy-based pan, then boil without stirring until the syrup turns a golden color (but do not allow it to darken or it will be bitter).

2. Pour the hot caramel into 6 x 5oz dariole molds, working quickly. Tilt each mold to ensure it is evenly lined on the bottom and a little way up the side with caramel, discard any excess, and allow the caramel to cool.

3. Bring the cream, milk, and maple syrup to simmering point in a pan over medium heat. Whisk the eggs and egg yolks in a bowl, then slowly pour in the hot cream, whisking continuously. Pour the cream mixture through a fine-mesh sieve into a large measuring jug, then carefully fill the prepared molds. Remove any surface bubbles using a teaspoon.

4. Place the molds in the slow cooker. Pour in boiling water to come three-quarters of the way up their sides, cover, and cook on low for 3–3½ hours.

5. Remove the lid and allow the creams to cool in the slow cooker, then take them out of the water, place on a tray, and cover in plastic wrap. Refrigerate for at least 5 hours before serving.

Make this in advance
This dessert can be made up to 2 days in advance.

SERVES
4

PREP
40 MINS

SOAK
30 MINS

COOKING
3–4 HRS

SETTING
HIGH

This is an upmarket bread-and-butter pudding using that lovely egg-rich brioche instead of plain leftover bread. The slow cooker produces excellent results with a perfect custard finish.

Marmalade-brioche baked custard

12oz brioche, cut to the shape of the terrine and into ½in slices to fit

7½ tbsp unsalted butter, softened, plus extra for greasing

12oz jar orange marmalade

2 pints heavy cream

2 cups full-fat milk

1 vanilla pod, split lengthways and seeds scraped out

juice and grated zest of 1 organic orange

⅓ cup Cointreau or Grand Marnier

4 eggs

6 egg yolks

1¼ cups superfine sugar, plus extra for sprinkling

to serve

ice cream or vanilla custard

1. Lightly butter a 9 x 5 x 3in terrine dish. Spread the brioche slices with the butter, then the marmalade, and arrange overlapping in several layers in the terrine. Place the cream, milk, and vanilla pod and seeds into a pan and bring to a boil, then remove from the heat and set aside.

2. Put the orange juice and zest, liqueur, eggs, egg yolks, and sugar into a large bowl and whisk until well combined. Then pour over the cream mixture, whisking continuously until smooth. Strain this custard over the brioche, then sprinkle with a little superfine sugar to coat the surface. Leave the brioche to soak up the custard for 30 minutes.

3. Place the terrine in the slow cooker and carefully pour boiling water around it to come halfway up the sides. Cover and cook on high for 3–4 hours, until just set.

4. Remove from the slow cooker and allow to rest for 15 minutes before serving with ice cream or vanilla custard.

SERVING SUGGESTION
If you wish, you can scatter the surface of the cooked pudding with a thin layer of superfine sugar and then glaze it with a blowtorch or under a very hot broiler.

Also try
Thinly slice a peeled organic orange and arrange the orange between the slices of brioche when layering the pudding.

SERVES
6–8

PREP
20 MINS

COOKING
3¼–4 HRS

SETTING
HIGH

This brings back memories of childhood. Every day we would indulge in a hot dessert and this was one of my favorites. Gone are the days of 2 hours' exercise every day, so dessert has become a rare treat for me.

Treacle sponge

3 tbsp corn syrup

1½ sticks unsalted butter, plus extra for greasing

1 tbsp fresh white breadcrumbs

juice of 1½ lemons

1 scant cup superfine sugar

grated zest of 1 unwaxed or organic lemon

3 eggs, beaten

1¾ cups self-rising flour

about 3 tbsp milk

to serve

custard or cream

1. Place the corn syrup in a buttered 5-cup pudding basin with the breadcrumbs and juice of ½ lemon.

2. To make the sponge: place the butter and sugar in a bowl and gently cream together until pale, using an electric whisk. Mix in the lemon zest and then slowly whisk in alternate spoonfuls of beaten egg and flour until both have been used up. Fold in the remainder of the lemon juice and just enough milk for the mixture to drop easily from the spoon.

3. Spoon the sponge mixture over the syrup in the pudding basin. Cover with a large disk of parchment paper, which you have pleated in the centre to allow the sponge room for expansion while it is cooking. Place a double-layer piece of buttered foil, also pleated, on top and secure with twine, making a handle so that you can easily lift the basin.

4. Place the pudding on an upturned plate or saucer inside your slow cooker, and pour in enough boiling water to come two-thirds up the side of the basin. Cover and cook on high for 3¼–4 hours, until a skewer comes out clean. Occasionally, as the water evaporates, add more with boiling water.

5. Remove the pudding basin from the slow cooker and allow to cool slightly. Cut away the twine and remove the foil and parchment paper. Invert the treacle sponge onto a serving plate, ensuring that all the syrup comes out of the bottom of the basin. Serve with custard or cream.

SERVES
6

PREP
20 MINS

SOAK
30 MINS

COOKING
2½ HRS

SETTING
HIGH

This is a sophisticated dessert that's a little unusual. A cross between savory and sweet, the dried fruit marries well with my favorite blue cheese, which is made locally to me, near Reading, in Berkshire.

Baked Lebanese fruit with melting blue cheese

3 tbsp unsalted butter, melted, plus extra for greasing

¾ cup dried figs, roughly chopped

1 scant cup dried apricots, cut into ¼in dice

½ cup Medjool dates, sliced

½ cup dried cherries

⅓ cup dried blueberries

¼ cup dried mixed citrus peel

¾ cup Orange Muscat or sweet wine

¾ cup water

½ tsp ground cinnamon

½ cup semolina

2 tsp clear honey

½ tsp orange flower water

6oz Barkham Blue cheese, (or other blue cheese) thinly sliced

1. Lightly butter 6 x 5oz dariole molds (small enough to fit into your slow cooker) and place in the fridge for the butter to set hard.

2. Mix together the dried fruit and peel and the Orange Muscat and leave to soak for 30 minutes, stirring from time to time.

3. Add all the other ingredients (except the cheese), and pour in ¾ cup water. Stir to combine. Fill each mold three-quarters full with the mixture.

4. Place the molds in the bottom of your slow cooker and then carefully pour hot water around them to come halfway up the sides. Cover and cook on high for 2½ hours until the fillings are set.

5. Turn them out onto a baking pan and top each with a slice or 2 of blue cheese. Place under a hot broiler, and when the cheese has melted, serve immediately.

Spiced apple terrine and honeyed yogurt

Slow cooking this unusual apple terrine is perfect for developing the natural appley flavors. I've used a combination of Cox's and my favorite Bramley apples, but feel free to play with whatever apple grabs your fancy.

1 scant cup superfine sugar

3²⁄₃lb all-purpose apples of your choice, peeled and cored

grated zest of 1 unwaxed or organic lemon

grated zest of 1 organic orange

2 tsp ground cinnamon

½ tsp ground star anise

½ cup flaked almonds, toasted

1 cup plain, strained yogurt

1 tbsp clear honey

1. Line an 8 x 4 x 2in terrine or loaf pan—or similar—with a layer of foil and a layer of nonstick parchment paper, allowing a 4in overhang on the long sides.

2. Combine half the sugar with 3 tbsp water in a small heavy-based pan over medium heat, allow the sugar to dissolve completely, then swirl around gently for another 6–8 minutes until the sugar has turned a pale golden color (but do not allow it to darken or it will be bitter). Pour the caramel into the base of the terrine and allow to cool.

3. Meanwhile, thinly slice the apples and toss with the zests. Mix the remaining sugar with the cinnamon and star anise, then toss with the apple and almonds.

4. Layer the apple mixture on top of the caramel in the terrine. Cover the apple mixture with the parchment paper and foil, then wrap the whole terrine in another layer of foil to enclose completely.

5. Place in the slow cooker and carefully pour boiling water into the slow cooker bowl to come halfway up the sides of the terrine. Cover with a lid and cook on low for 8 hours. Cool, place a weight on the terrine to press the contents down, and refrigerate overnight.

6. Combine the yogurt and honey, and refrigerate until needed.

7. To serve, gently tip the terrine onto a platter, remove the wrappings, and carefully cut into 1in slices using a serrated knife or, ideally, an electric carving knife. Serve with the honeyed yogurt.

Make this in advance
You can make the terrine at least 24 hours ahead—it will keep for 1 week.

SERVES
4

PREP
15 MINS

COOKING
4 HRS

SETTING
HIGH &
LOW

Rome Beauty is the apple of choice for whole baked apples and, with slow cooking, you won't have the problem of bursting apples.

Baked fruit and nut apples

6½ tbsp unsalted butter, at room temperature

⅓ cup cranberry juice

4 large Rome Beauty apples, cored

½ cup dark muscovado sugar

grated zest and juice of 1 organic orange

grated zest of 1 unwaxed or organic lemon

¼ tsp apple pie spice mix

3 tbsp well-crushed amaretti cookies

⅓ cup macadamia nuts, roughly chopped

¼ cup dried cranberries

1 tbsp mincemeat (see page 214)

2 tbsp amaretto liqueur

to serve

English Double Devon cream or custard

1. Grease the slow-cooker ceramic pot with 1½ tbsp of the butter, then pour in the cranberry juice, cover, and turn the cooker to high.

2. With a melon baller or teaspoon, enlarge the apple cavity to twice its size. Run the tip of a sharp knife skin deep around the circumference of each apple.

3. Put the remaining butter, sugar, citrus zests and juice, spice, and crushed cookies in a bowl and combine together with a wooden spoon. Then add all the remaining ingredients, except the apples.

4. Divide the mixture between the apples, filling the cavities completely and piling any excess on top of the apples. Stand the apples upright in the slow cooker, cover, and reduce the temperature to low, then cook for 4 hours, until the apples are tender.

5. Transfer the apples to 4 warm bowls with any excess filling and the juices. Serve with English Double Devon cream or custard.

Apple pie spice
If you can't find apple pie spice in the grocery store, combine 1 tbsp ground cinnamon, ½ tsp grated fresh nutmeg, 1 tsp ground allspice, and ¼ tsp ground cloves. It will keep for months in an airtight jar.

SERVES
4

PREP
45 MINS

COOKING
8¼–10¼
HRS

SETTING
LOW

Quince is a fruit you rarely see on sale in the grocery store, but as it is such a delicious fruit, it's well worth making a detour to find some in the fall. Shaped like a very hard yellow pear, it takes a lot of cooking, but it does have a magical perfume and unique flavor.

Poached quince with vanilla yogurt mousse

for the poached quince

2 ⅔ cups superfine sugar

1 ¼ cups Marsala or sweet sherry

½ vanilla pod, split lengthways

½ cinnamon stick

½ tsp mixed spice

1 bay leaf

1 thyme sprig

2 large quinces

1 strip of unwaxed or organic orange rind

for the yogurt mousse

2 gelatin leaves

1 ¾ cups heavy cream

scant ½ cup superfine sugar

1 vanilla pod, split lengthways

1 ¼ cups plain, strained yogurt

1. To poach the quinces, first place the sugar, 2½ pints water, Marsala, spices, bay leaf, and thyme in a pan and bring to a gentle boil. Simmer for 5 minutes, until the sugar has dissolved and the liquid is clear.

2. Peel and halve the quinces, retaining the peel. Pour the poaching liquid into your slow cooker with the orange rind, quince halves, and peel. Ensure the quinces are covered with liquid—add a layer of wet crumpled parchment paper to keep the fruit submerged—cover, and cook on low for 8–10 hours until the fruit is tender, adding boiling water as necessary.

3. Meanwhile, to make the mousse, soak the gelatin in cold water for 8 minutes without stirring. Drain.

4. Gently heat half the cream with the sugar and vanilla pod in a pan to just under boiling, stirring to dissolve the sugar. Remove from the heat and stir in the gelatin to melt. Allow to cool (but not get cold or the gelatin will set), then strain through a sieve into a bowl.

5. Fold in the yogurt and whisk to emulsify. Whisk the remaining cream until ribboning, then fold into the yogurt mix. Refrigerate until needed.

6. Remove the cooked quinces from the poaching liquor, then cut out the core from the center of each quince half.

7. Strain the poaching liquor into a saucepan and boil over fierce heat for 10–12 minutes, until it becomes a sticky syrup. Allow the syrup to cool to room temperature.

8. Place a quince half in each bowl, spoon a dollop of mousse into its center, and drizzle over a little spiced syrup.

SERVES
4

PREP
15 MINS

SOAK
30 MINS

COOKING
1½ HRS

SETTING
HIGH

The more I go to Jamaica, the more I'm inspired by their simple use of indigenous ingredients. The freshest of fish, the wonderful jerk (traditional spice rub for meat), and perfectly ripened tropical fruit. Here I'm using that highly popular fruit, the banana.

Jamaican coconut bananas

½ cup California golden raisins

⅓ cup dark rum

½ cup coconut milk

4¼ tbsp unsalted butter, diced

scant ½ cup dark muscovado sugar

4 yellow (but not overripe) bananas, peeled and halved lengthways

pinch of grated nutmeg

pinch of ground allspice

⅓ cup heavy cream

½ cup fresh coconut flakes

to serve

rum and raisin ice cream

1. Soak the golden raisins in the rum for 30 minutes.

2. Place the coconut milk, butter, sugar, golden raisins, and rum in the slow cooker on high and leave, uncovered, for 30 minutes, until the butter and sugar have melted, then stir to combine.

3. Add the bananas, cover, and cook on high for 40 minutes, turning the bananas once. Sprinkle with the spices, add the cream, and stir to combine. Cover and cook for a further 20 minutes.

4. Carefully lift the bananas onto 4 warm plates. Spoon over the sauce and sprinkle with the coconut flakes. Serve hot with rum and raisin ice-cream.

SERVING SUGGESTION
Toast the coconut flakes, if you like, in a dry skillet over medium heat, until just turning brown, but beware because they burn easily. Some supermarkets sell prepared, ready-peeled fresh coconut, so you could create your own flakes using a vegetable peeler.

SERVES 4

PREP 15 MINS

COOKING 2–3 HRS

SETTING LOW

Lucky man that I am, I have a fig tree … in Spain. And I've found that figs work like magic in my slow cooker and don't show much sign of shrinkage.

Poached figs with blackberries

2 cups blackberries, defrosted if frozen
juice of 1 orange
juice of 2 lemons
heaping ½ cup superfine sugar
2 tbsp crème de cassis (optional)
12 fresh figs

to decorate
a few mint leaves (optional)

to serve
1 cup crème fraîche
2 tbsp finely chopped mint
1 tbsp clear honey

1. Purée the blackberries with the orange juice in a food processor or liquidizer until smooth, then press through a sieve and discard the seeds. Gently heat the lemon juice and sugar in a small pan, stirring until the sugar has dissolved.

2. Stir the blackberry purée and cassis, if using, into the lemon syrup, then pour into the slow cooker. Add the figs, cover, and cook on low for 2–3 hours.

3. Meanwhile, mix the crème fraîche with the chopped mint and honey and spoon into a small serving bowl. Refrigerate until needed.

4. Serve the figs while still warm or transfer to a glass dish and chill. Sprinkle with extra mint leaves, if you like, and serve with spoonfuls of the crème fraîche.

Also try
Halved peaches with a raspberry Melba sauce would also be great cooked this way.

You could also try stirring a little chopped stem ginger into the crème fraîche instead of the mint and honey.

SERVES
4

PREP
25 MINS +
REFRIGERATE
3 HRS

COOKING
3–4 HRS

SETTING
LOW

You've got a double whammy here: a perfect breakfast dish or a grown-up dessert.
If you're not a fan of prunes, just leave them out or substitute some other dried fruit.

Compote of pears, prunes, oranges, and walnuts in spiced wine

4 Bartlett pears, peeled and halved with the stems left intact

2 organic oranges

8 Agen prunes

16 walnut halves

for the spiced wine

2 cups red Beaujolais

heaping ½ cup superfine sugar

6 black peppercorns

pinch of grated fresh nutmeg

pinch of ground cinnamon

½ tsp coriander seeds, toasted

1 clove

2 bay leaves

½ vanilla pod, slit lengthways

pared rind and juice of ½ organic orange

juice of ½ lemon

2 tbsp redcurrant jelly

2 thin slices of fresh ginger

to serve

vanilla ice cream (optional)

1. Combine all the ingredients for the spiced wine in a saucepan and bring just to a boil. Remove and keep warm over the lowest heat.

2. Remove the cores from the pears using a teaspoon or melon baller, then nestle them closely together in the base of the slow cooker. Pour the wine mixture over the top, making sure that the pears are submerged as much as possible using a layer of crumpled, wet parchment paper. Cover and cook on low for 3–4 hours until the pears are tender.

3. Lift the pears out of the wine and transfer to a glass dish. Peel and de-pith the oranges, then slice each one into 6 horizontally, removing any seeds. Add to the pears with the prunes and walnut halves.

4. Strain the wine mixture, if you like, over the pears. Leave to cool, then chill in the fridge for 3 hours. Serve on its own or with scoops of good vanilla ice cream.

SERVING SUGGESTION
This tastes wonderful with home-made cinnamon ice cream. Or, you could use regular vanilla ice cream but sprinkle a little ground cinnamon over it just before serving.

To make a thicker sauce
If you would like the spiced wine to be thicker, pour the liquid into a wide pan at the end of the pear cooking time. Boil rapidly for 5 minutes until reduced by about one-third, then pour over the pears and leave to cool.

SERVES
4

PREP
25 MINS

COOKING
1¾–2½ HRS

SETTING
HIGH

Blue cheese, pears, sweet wine, and Roquefort—you just can't go wrong with this combo. It's great as an appteizer or even as a cheese course. Serve hot or at room temperature.

Braised pear with Roquefort

4 barely ripe Bartlett or Anjou
   pears, peeled, cored, and halved
   vertically

¼ cup ricotta

¼ cup Roquefort

½ carrot, finely diced

½ celery stalk, finely diced

4 Medjool dates, stoned and diced

1 tbsp clear honey

¼ tsp sweet paprika

⅔ cup sweet white wine
   (Orange Muscat or Beaumes
   de Venise)

freshly ground black pepper

pinch of grated nutmeg

pinch of ground cinnamon

5 tbsp finely chopped walnuts

to serve

salad leaves

8oz wedge of Roquefort

1. Place the pears, cut-side up, on a cutting board. Hollow out a little of the center of each with a teaspoon or melon baller.

2. Combine the ricotta, Roquefort, carrot, celery, dates, honey, and paprika in a bowl. Spoon the mixture into the pear cavities and place the pears, filling-side up, in the base of the slow cooker.

3. Carefully pour the sweet wine around the pears and then sprinkle them with the pepper, nutmeg, and cinnamon. Cover and cook on high for 1¾–2½ hours until the pears are tender.

4. Remove the pears carefully to a baking pan and place under a hot broiler to brown.

5. Sprinkle with the walnuts and serve with some of the juices, dressed salad leaves, and a wedge of Roquefort.

SERVES
8–10

PREP
40 MINS

COOKING
4–5 HRS

SETTING
HIGH

Carrot cakes are always a hit, but this one has a little more going on, with big flavors and lovely textures.

Spiced carrot cake with cream-cheese frosting

unsalted butter, for greasing

3 cups self-rising flour

2 tsp baking powder

½ tbsp ground cinnamon

½ tsp grated fresh nutmeg

½ tsp ground allspice

grated zest of 1 unwaxed orange

1 scant cup soft dark brown sugar

¾ cup olive oil

3 large eggs, lightly beaten

1½ cups cooked carrots, puréed

1 carrot, grated

¾ cup walnuts, finely chopped

½ cup raisins

⅔ cup desiccated coconut

¼ cup canned crushed pineapple in juice, drained

for the cream-cheese frosting

½ cup cream cheese or
  ⅔ cup mascarpone

2 cups confectioners' sugar

7 tbsp unsalted butter, softened

½ tsp vanilla extract

juice of ½ lemon

1. Butter a 7in round cake pan and line with nonstick parchment paper. Turn the slow cooker to high and pour in 1in water. Put an upturned saucer or plate in the bottom of the slow cooker.

2. Sift together the flour, baking powder, cinnamon, nutmeg, and allspice. Fold in the orange zest and brown sugar and combine well.

3. Add the oil, eggs, carrot purée, grated carrot, walnuts, raisins, coconut, and pineapple to the dry ingredients and fold to combine, but don't overwork it.

4. Pour the mixture into the lined pan and level the surface. Place in the slow cooker and pour in more boiling water to come halfway up the sides of the pan. Cover and cook on high for 4–5, hours until the edge of the cake pulls away from the side of the pan, and a skewer inserted in the center comes out clean.

5. Meanwhile, make the cream-cheese frosting in a food processor. Blend all the ingredients together until smooth.

6. Remove the cake pan from the slow cooker. Leave the cake to cool in the pan for 15 minutes, then turn out onto a cake rack, remove the parchment paper, and allow to cool completely.

7. Spread the cream-cheese frosting on the top and side of the cake.

Choosing your pan
If you prefer, use a more traditional loaf pan or terrine mold, but make sure it holds the same quantity as the one used in the recipe. The cooking time remains the same.

Why buy jars of bland mincemeat when it's so easy to make your own? This one even has the added thrill of proper booze. And, by slow cooking, you lengthen the shelf-life of the unopened product.

A Christmas quantity of classic mincemeat

¾ cup dark rum

1¼ cups dry sherry

3⅓ cups mixed dried currants, raisins, and golden raisins

1lb 2oz all-purpose apples, peeled, cored, and finely chopped or coarsely grated

1lb 2oz shredded beef or vegetarian suet

1 cup flaked almonds, roughly chopped

¾ cup dried apricots, finely chopped

2¼ cups light muscovado sugar

1 tsp ground cinnamon

pinch of grated nutmeg

1½ tsp mixed spice

grated zest and juice of 1 unwaxed or organic lemon

grated zest and juice of 1 organic orange

2 tsp ground ginger

1 heaping cup mixed candied peel, finely chopped

½ cup glacé cherries, quartered

1. Mix half the rum and half the sherry in a large bowl with all the other ingredients, cover with plastic wrap and leave for a day or so for the flavors to develop.

2. When ready, place the mincemeat in your slow cooker, cover, and cook on high for 1 hour. Stir well. Reduce the heat to low, cover, and cook for a further 2 hours, stirring halfway. Leave the mixture to cool completely, then fold in the remaining alcohol.

3. Pack the mincemeat into warm, sterilized jars (see opposite), and seal with wax-paper disks and tight-fitting lids.

4. The mincemeat will keep for up to 6 months in a cool, dry place, but once opened, store in the fridge for up to 4 weeks.

MAKES
1lb 2oz

PREP
20 MINS

COOKING
2 HRS

SETTING
LOW

This is one of my favorite spreads for toast, but this is not your only option. Try lemon curd mixed with crumbled meringues and whipped cream; or meringue nests topped with whipped cream and a piping of lemon curd; or use it as a sponge-cake filling.

A pleasant lemon curd

grated zest and juice of 3 unwaxed
   or organic lemons

7½ tbsp unsalted butter, diced

1 cup superfine sugar

2 large eggs and 2 yolks, beaten

1. Place the lemon zest and juice, butter, and sugar in a nonstick pan and heat gently for 2–3 minutes, until the butter has melted, stirring from time to time. Pour into a bowl, then put this on an upturned saucer placed in the bottom of your slow cooker.

2. Strain the eggs and yolks through a sieve, add to the lemon mixture, and stir well. Cover the bowl with foil (just pressed over the top), pour hot water to come halfway up the side of the bowl, cover, and cook on low for 2 hours, until very thick. Stir once or twice during the cooking process.

3. Pour into small, warm, sterilized jars (see below), then cover the lemon curd with wax-paper disks and tight-fitting lids. Store in the fridge for up to 6 months.

How to sterilize jam jars
Sterilize jars by heating them in the oven at 300°F for 20 minutes, then turn off the heat, and allow the jars to cool slightly before putting the preserve into them. Alternatively, soak the jars in sterilizing solution, rinse the jars, and put them into the oven to dry out. I find it easiest to have all the jars on a tray and then, using a ladle, transfer the hot jam or curd into a large measuring jug before pouring it into the hot jars.

Stocks

MAKES
3 PINT)

PREP
15 MINS

COOKING
8–10 HRS

SETTING
HIGH

The perfect chicken stock

1 roast chicken carcass, chopped

1lb 2oz chicken wings, chopped

2 whole onions, spiked with 2 cloves each

1 carrot, thinly sliced

2 garlic cloves, crushed

1 celery stalk, sliced

whites of 2 leeks, sliced

½ bunch of parsley, leaves and stalks

1 bouquet garni

½ bottle dry white wine

1 tsp white peppercorns, crushed

salt and freshly ground black pepper

1. Put the carcass and chicken wings in your slow cooker and add hot water to cover. Add all the remaining ingredients and cook on high, covered, for 8–10 hours, skimming every couple of hours. Add more water to fill it back up, if needed. Season to taste.

2. Strain through a fine sieve and leave to settle. Remove the fat, skimming off the last traces with a paper towel.

3. Store in the fridge for up to 4 days or freeze (see tip opposite).

MAKES
2 CUPS

PREP
15 MINS

COOKING
8–10 HRS

SETTING
LOW

The perfect vegetable stock

2 carrots, roughly chopped

2 onions, quartered

2 celery stalks, roughly chopped

½ fennel bulb, roughly chopped

2 leeks, roughly chopped

4 tomatoes, roughly chopped

8 button mushrooms, quartered

1 tsp black peppercorns

2 dried bay leaves

3 parsley stalks

2 thyme sprigs

1. Place all the ingredients in the slow cooker and cover with hot water. Cook on low for 8–10 hours. Strain into a large bowl and leave to cool.

2. Store in the fridge for up to 3 days or freeze (see below).

Freezing stock
To freeze, halve the stock by boiling it vigorously until it has reduced, then cool. Pour into ice-cube trays and freeze. When they have frozen, place the cubes into a labeled plastic freezer bag and use as required by placing in a jug and adding boiling water to dissolve.

Acknowledgments

My great appreciation and fondness to Rebecca Spry for commissioning this book and for her good humor and tenacity throughout; an iron hand in a velvet glove.

Thanks also must go to Diona Murray, who diligently plowed through my recipes, honed, and gilded them; Elizabeth Zeschin who always does my recipes justice, one of the best food photographers around; Yasia Willams-Leedham and Juliette Norsworthy for putting together such a great design; and Georgina Atsiaris, my book editor, whose behind-the-scenes skills are always top-notch.

I must mention the constant support and encouragement of my brilliant wife, Jacinta and our children, Toby and Billie.

Finally, my thanks to Louise Townsend, my ultra-efficient PA, who was constantly on hand when the pressures of deadlines occasionally took their toll, and to Fiona Lindsay my agent, and her team at Limelight Management, who provided their usual expertise and support.